SCROLL SAW

Picture Frames

SO-AXO-973

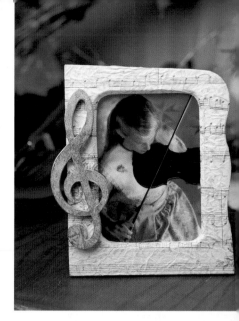

SCROLL SAW

Picture Frames

Patrick Spielman

Sterling Publishing Co., Inc. New York
A Sterling/Chapelle Book

Chapelle Ltd.

Owner: Jo Packham
Design/layout Editor: Leslie Ridenour
Photographer: Kevin Dilley for Hazen Photography

Staff: Marie Barber, Ann Bear, Areta Bingham, Kass Burchett, Rebecca Christensen, Holly Fuller, Marilyn Goff, Shirley Heslop, Holly Hollingsworth, Sherry Hoppe, Shawn Hsu, Susan Jorgensen, Pauline Locke, Barbara Milburn, Linda Orton, Karmen Quinney, Cindy Stoeckl

If you have any questions or comments or would like information about any specialty products featured in this book, please contact:

Chapelle Ltd., Inc.
P.O. Box 9252
Ogden, UT 84409

Phone: (801) 621-2777
FAX: (801) 621-2788
e-mail: Chapelle1@aol.com

Library of Congress Cataloging-in-Publication Data Available

10 9 8 7 6 5 4 3 2 1

A Sterling/Chapelle Book

Published by Sterling Publishing Company, Inc.
387 Park Avenue South, New York, NY 10016
© 1999 by Chapelle Ltd.
Distributed in Canada by Sterling Publishing
% Canadian Manda Group, ONe Atlantic Avenue, Suite 105
Toronto, Ontartio, Canada M6K 3E7
Distributed in Great Britain and Europe by Cassell PLC
Wellington House, 125 Strand, London WC2R 0BB, England
Distributed in Australia by Capricorn Link (Australia) Pty Ltd.
P.O. Box 6651, Baulkham Hills, Business Centre, NSW 2153, Australia
Printed in China
All Rights Reserved

Sterling ISBN 0-8069-0311-2

Due to the limited amount of space available, we must print our patterns at a reduced size in order to give our patrons the maximum number of projects possible in our publications. We believe the quality and quantity of our patterns will compensate for any inconvenience this may cause.

The written instructions, photographs, designs, patterns, and projects in this volume are intended for the personal use of the reader and may be reproduced for that purpose only. Any other use, especially commercial use, is forbidden under law without the written permission of the copyright holder.

Every effort has been made to ensure that all of the information in this book is accurate. However, due to differing conditions, tools, and individual skills, the publisher cannot be responsible for any injuries, losses, and/or any other damages which may result from the use of the information in this book.

Contents

Introduction

Picture framing is not what it used to be. Typically, frames have been made from specially shaped stick mouldings, with their ends mitered and assembled at the corners. Today, new technology and unusual designs combine to create frames that border on works of art in and of themselves.

Commercially produced frames are made from a variety of materials and are available in a wide range of designs with an endless choice of finishes and colors. Large scale manufacturers have recently been capitalizing on a popular factory technique called laser cutting. This expensive process quickly produces extremely ornamental and highly detailed surfaces.

The do-it-yourself answer to laser produced frames is America's most popular woodworking tool—the modern scroll saw. Actually, because frames cut on the scroll saw are individually made, they are even more distinctive as they do not have the same common characteristics as do laser cut frames that are produced in large quantities.

For those new to the present day craft of scroll sawing, some introductory topics are highlighted relative to making the frame projects in this book. For those who already have some experience with the scroll saw, there are more than 30 patterns with basic how-to instructions for making frames that range from easy to exquisite. Many of these frames can be completed in one afternoon. Loved ones' photos deserve to be displayed with pride in these hand-crafted frames.

Patrick Spielman, 1999

General Information

Wood Materials

As is evident from the variety of frames in this book, a broad range of materials with different characteristics have been used: soft to hard, light to dark, inexpensive to expensive, thin to thick, common to exotic, natural to painted, and so on. When making wood choices for frame projects, it is important to keep in mind a few considerations.

Solid wood is categorized as hardwood or softwood. The best choice of any wood is, by and large, dictated by the specific end use. Sometimes physical hardness is important; however, it is not a major consideration for photo frames. Common hardwoods include ash, beech, birch, cherry, maple, oak, and pecan. Mahogany, poplar, and walnut might be considered medium-hard. Typical softwoods include basswood, butternut, cedars, cypress, firs, pines, redwood, and spruce. *See Photos No. 1 and No. 2.* Then there are the exotic woods such as paduk, purpleheart, zebra, and many others. Most exotic woods are considered to be hard rather than soft and are almost always quite expensive.

When a natural finish is desired, woods should be selected for their color and figure or grain patterns. It is important to understand that different grain patterns result from the way the board is cut from the log. *See Photo No. 1.* If the frame will be stained or painted, any wood will serve. However, the prudent choice is an inexpensive softwood or a re-manufactured sheet material, such as plywood.

The various materials as shown in the photos of this book are, in fact, only a small

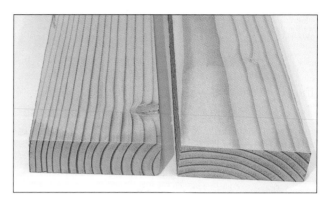

Photo No. 1. A general rule for all woods: Quarter-sawn boards, like the one on the left, will stay flatter and distort less than the plain-sawn boards on the right. Note the different grain patterns from the growth rings. These examples are of Douglas Fir—not a recommended choice for picture framing because it tends to splinter and it is also difficult to smooth.

Photo No. 2. Inexpensive No. 2 shop pine is sometimes a good choice for small projects that can be cut out around defects. Boards may be found flat like the one on the left, but usually wide plain-sawn boards will have some distortion and cupping, like the boards at the lower right. Note the typical knot and pitch pockets, which are areas that should be avoided.

sampling of suitable materials available. Check with a local supplier for available species, pricing, and other options.

Tips: *Purchasing less costly, lower grades of wood justifies cutting from clear areas between defects. Consider the possibility of positioning patterns around problem areas, such as knots, so they are removed when cutting inside openings. Discolored boards (blue-stain, etc.) are fine to use when a frame will be painted—as long as there is no decay—as their surfaces will be hidden anyway.*

As a general rule, avoid firs and cedars because they splinter easily and produce uneven surfaces when sanded. See Photo No. 1. Also, avoid pressure-treated yellow or southern pine, as they produce dangerous fumes and sawdust.

Plywood & Sheet Materials

Some plywoods and certain sheet materials offer advantages over solid boards. They do not check or crack. They stay flat, are strong in all directions, do not swell or shrink, and are available in larger sizes. Generally, they also have uniform surface characteristics with minimal waste. However, as a rule, sheet materials manufactured for utility work and building construction should not be used for scroll saw frame projects.

Some sheet materials cost less than solid woods, but others, such as fine hardwood plywoods, can be extremely expensive. Highly ornate and delicate designs are less fragile when sawn from plywood. Baltic birch plywoods, for example, have sound inner plies and are a popular choice for fretwork frames and general scroll saw work. *See Photo No. 3.*

MDF (medium density fiberboard) is not commonly used, but it is a good choice for painted frames, if it can be found. A building products supplier may be able to order a

4' x 8' sheet or maybe scraps can be obtained from a local cabinet maker. MDF is fairly inexpensive. It costs about half the price of No. 2 shop pine. It is a bit harder on saw blades and it also generates fine dust when cut, so always wear a dust mask. MDF is manufactured from lumbering leftovers of sawdust and chips. *See Photo No. 3 and refer to Photos No. 13 on page 16 and No. 17 on page 18.*

Photo No. 3. Left: Poplar plywoods and Baltic birch plywoods, in thinner sheets, are good for scroll sawing because of their void-free interiors and smooth surfaces. Baltic birch plywood thicker than ⅜" may cause blade dulling problems because of the abrasiveness of all the glue used to make up the board. Right: MDF (medium density fiberboard).

Scroll Saws

When compared to all other power driven devices that cut wood, the scroll saw is unquestionably the safest, most user-friendly, and easiest to master. Scroll sawing is enjoyed by crafters and artists of all ages. It requires no mechanical skills and it allows for safely cutting small pieces of wood to quickly make a variety of projects. The major function of the scroll saw is to cut irregular curves and openings in flat wood. A very small, narrow blade is held taut between the ends of two horizontal arms that move in unison up and down to create a reciprocating cutting motion. *See Photos No. 4 and No. 5.*

Photo No. 4. Scroll saws carry narrow blades. Although narrower blades than these are available, you will not need any finer than these. A general rule: Use wider blades with fewer teeth for sawing larger curves and cutting thicker woods; use narrower blades with more teeth for intricate details in thin woods.

Photo No. 5. Blades are clamped at each end to the upper arm, and to the lower arm under the table. An important feature of scroll saw usage is its capability for installing and changing blades quickly and easily.

The blade moves vertically through an opening in the saw table. The operator supports the work piece on the table and advances it into the blade in a manner that is similar to feeding fabric under the needle of a sewing machine.

Because of the very narrow blades, extremely sharp arcs and turns can be cut to make highly detailed and intricate objects. To the uneducated and untrained eye, many people think that scroll work was created with a laser. Scroll saws are available in a wide variety of prices, ranging from less than $100.00 to over $2,000.00, with a growing list of features and options that improve the overall performance of the machine. Many projects in this book can be made using any scroll saw, including the least expensive. There are many brands to choose from and some manufacturers offer several models. Before purchasing any scroll saw, seriously consider the full range of work that might be done in the future. Scroll saws can cut a wide variety of materials, including various metals and plastics. Some scroll saws have more capability and capacity to saw thicker and larger sizes of wood than do others. Thus, it is necessary to investigate and try various saws, to see which saw best matches long-term sawing needs. For a more in-depth description of scroll saw usage and features, the previously published Sterling books *Scroll Saw Basics* and *Scroll Saw Handbook* are recommended.

The size of the scroll saw is designated by its "throat capacity." This is the distance from the blade to the rear of the machine. A 15" saw, for example, can cut to the center of a 30"-diameter circle. Saw sizes range from 13" to 30" and are available in bench and floor model versions.

The rate at which the blade moves up and down in strokes per minute is called the "blade speed." The least expensive saws have just one constant speed. Two-speed and variable-speed saws allow for better control when cutting thin or soft materials, as well as the ability to efficiently cut metal and plastic.

The photos included here provide a good overview of some popular brands of saws that are currently available. *See Photos No. 6–8 and No. 9 on page 12.*

Photo No. 7. Hegner's 18" variable-speed features up-front tensioning. The cost is approximately $1,000.00.

Photo No. 6. Delta's two-speed 16" scroll saw is one of several models available from the manufacturer. The cost is approximately $175.00.

Photo No. 8. De Walt's 20" variable-speed saw is one of the newest brands available with many innovative features. The cost is approximately $475.00.

Photo No. 9. Excalibur's 30" variable-speed has the largest throat capacity available. The cost is approximately $1,400.00.

In addition to considering variable-speed saws, some saw features worth considering are up-front controls, i.e.: blade tensioning, on-off switch, and blade speed adjustment. Look into adaptability, i.e.: adding a light, a magnifier, a dust collector, and/or a blower. A foot switch is a good optional accessory. Remember, the most important feature to look for is its capacity for changing blades quickly and/or threading the blade through the work piece easily for making inside cuts. *See Photo No. 5 on page 10.*

Blades

Blades are fairly inexpensive, costing between 20 cents to 75 cents each, depending upon size, style, quantity, and quality. The most popular blade is the 5" plain-end type. Sizes are designated by numbers and range from Nos. 2/0 and 0 in very fine, to Nos. 1, 2, and 4 in fine, to Nos. 5 to 7 in medium, and Nos. 8 to 12 in large sizes. *Photo No. 4 on page 10 illustrates some medium- and fine-sized blades.*

The slight front to back movement of the blade during the cutting stroke of the scroll saw produces a sawn surface that is smooth and seldom needs sanding.

There are various blade tooth design configurations available, with skip-tooth being one of the most popular. *See Drawing No. 1.*

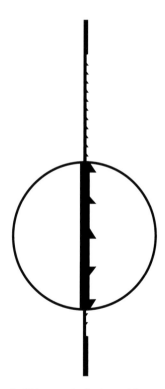

Drawing No. 1. Skip-tooth design with reversed lower teeth minimizes bottom splintering or feathering along the cut edges of the piece.

This blade tooth design provides for fast sawdust removal and provides cool and smooth cuts. Look for blades with reversed lower teeth. These minimize tear-out or splintering as the teeth exit the bottom of the work piece.

Less expensive blades have burr edges along one side. *See Drawing No. 2.* The burr edge is the result of material flow from stamping or milling during manufacturing. The burr-edged side of the blade is sharper and provides less cutting resistance than the burrless side of the blade. This causes the blade to track

slightly to one side while cutting—a condition for which one can quickly learn to compensate.

The side-tracking tendency of these blades is especially noticeable when making straight line cuts. *See Photo No. 10.*

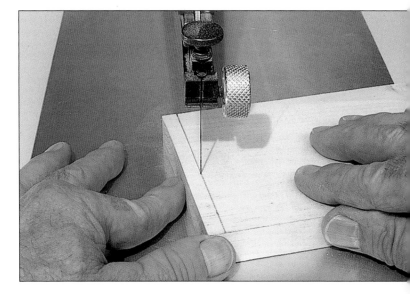

Photo No. 10. Practice straight-line cutting parallel to an edge. The feed direction here appears to be somewhat angular, and it actually is. This is because of the type of blade being used. It has a burr edge on the right side of the blade, resulting from the blade manufacturing process. Ground blades are uniformly sharp on both sides of the blade and do not require this compensation adjustment in feed directions.

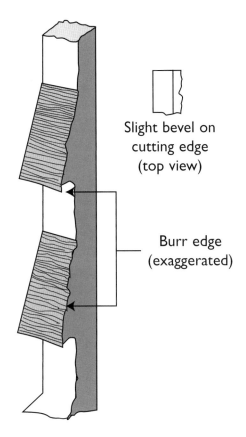

Slight bevel on cutting edge (top view)

Burr edge (exaggerated)

Drawing No. 2. This enlarged sketch shows the sharp, microscopic metal burr along one edge of the blade. This condition is typical of less expensive scroll saw blades. It is caused by the way blades are manufactured. For this reason, scroll saw blades actually track unevenly, because there is more cutting resistance on one edge of the blade than the other.

The best, newest, and most expensive blades are ground from tempered steel with abrasive wheels. These are known as "ground blades." They last longer and cut straighter when compared to other blades.

For general softwood cutting, use larger blades: Nos. 7 to 12 for ¾" and thicker stock. Use Nos. 5 to 7 for ½" to ¾" stock, and Nos. 1 to 5 for ⅛" to ½" stock. Just three blades—No. 4, No. 7, and No. 9—are recommended to handle most of the cutting projects in this book.

Use ground blades for the smoothest-sawn surfaces. They stay sharp longer when cutting plywoods and also make smooth cuts in pine.

Avoid spiral blades. Although designed to cut in all directions, they are not a good choice for beginners. They cut slowly and leave a very rough-sawn surface.

Preparing Saws

Make certain to first read and review the owner's manual and observe all of the safety precautions relative to the use of the scroll saw. For most of the projects, it is necessary to make cuts with the saw table set square to the blade. Use a small square or a protractor to make and check this adjustment. The factory calibrations on the blade-tilt scales of most scroll saws are difficult to read (especially with bifocals) and most are not accurate. *See Photo No. 11.*

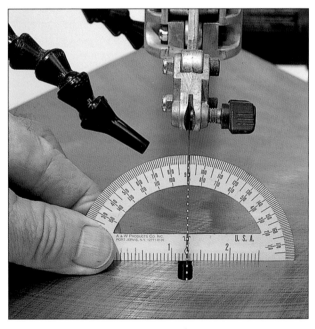

Photo No. 11. Using a simple protractor as shown, is the easiest way to check the squareness of the table to the blade and to adjust table tilt to the desired angle for bevel cutting.

Make certain that the blade is installed with the teeth pointing downward. Tension it correctly, according to the manufacturer's instructions. For beginners, making some preliminary cuts is recommended until confidence is gained and various lines can be followed consistently. The most difficult types of cuts to make accurately are: perfectly straight lines, a true radius or full circle, and other geometric shapes, such as ovals, squares, and any parallel lines that run close together. *See Photo No. 10 on page 13.* Patience and practice are the keys to developing sawing skills.

Beginners should also use the hold-down and guard. Making quick, sharp "on-the-spot" turns to cut inside corners and acute angles requires some practice and a fairly narrow blade. There are alternative techniques for successfully making these cuts. One method is accomplished by sawing into the corner and then backing up the work piece and making one or more short cuts to widen the saw cut or kerf. This permits the work piece to be turned without twisting the blade.

Many projects have inside openings that must be cut away. Simply drill a small hole in the waste area. Thread the blade through the work piece, reattach it to the saw, and begin cutting.

For most projects, the pattern provides cutting lines to follow. It does not matter if the cut is directly on the line or slightly to one side of it. However, cutting too far outside the line may spoil the integrity of the design.

Tips: Plywoods that are ¼" and thinner are not easy to cut unless cut on a slow-speed saw. If a slow-speed saw is not available, add extra stability to the project by using a waste-backer nailed, glued, or affixed with double-sided tape under the work piece. A waste-backer adds "blade resistance," resulting in better sawing control. The waste-backer also minimizes tear-out and splintering on the bottom of the work piece. Used plywood or paneling makes an effective, yet inexpensive waste-backer material.

A waste-backer can be secured under the work piece with nails, which, in many cases, is better than using messy double-sided tape. Drive small brads through the waste areas of both pieces while held over a flat piece of metal. The metal will peen the nails on the bottom side. This technique works well with plywoods even as thin as $\frac{1}{32}$" thick.

The same techniques can be employed when stack cutting. Stack cutting is a good production technique. It involves placing two or more layers, one on top of the other, securing them together so they don't slip or shift, and sawing all layers at once.

Preparing Patterns

Measure the photo or artwork that will be framed and compare it to the opening sizes given for the patterns. Cropping the photo, if possible, may be advantageous. Determine if the patterns will be used as presented in the book or if adjustments need to be made. Each pattern can be reduced or enlarged to any size desired at a copy shop or with an office photocopy machine. Consider also the sizes of wood materials either on hand or needing to be purchased for the frame project(s) selected. A slight size reduction of the frame pattern may allow for fitting it onto a piece of wood that would otherwise be cast aside.

Use a proportion scale to help determine the exact percentage of reduction or enlargement required before making a photocopy of the frame pattern. See Photo No. 12. Select the wood. Sand and smooth the surface and remove excess dust with a tack cloth.

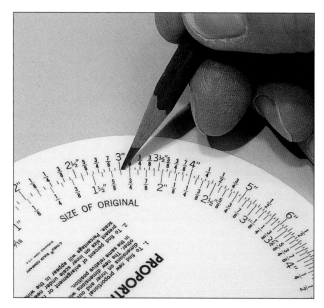

Photo No. 12. A proportion scale is used to determine optimum sizes when reducing or enlarging patterns on a photocopy machine. Simply align the mark indicating the existing size of the pattern in the book, then turn the scale to the desired finished size and take note of the percentage in the window. Set the copy machine to the percentage designated in the proportion scale's window.

Using scissors, cut the excess paper from around the copy of the pattern, leaving about $\frac{1}{2}$" beyond the shape of the design. The wood should be slightly larger than the copy. Spray the back of the copy with a temporary bonding aerosol spray adhesive, such as 3M's Spray Mount®. Allow it to dry about 30 seconds and hand press the copy to the face surface of the wooden work piece. The workpiece is now ready for sawing.

Using a Router

Some instructions specify the use of a router for completing basic edge work. This includes machining a rabbet cut (lip) into the back edge for mounting the photo or artwork.

A router is also convenient for forming decorative edges, such as round-overs and chamfers. Combining the use of the scroll saw with fundamental router operations creates some truly stunning and professional frames. For those who are not experienced with the router, the book, *Router Basics,* published by Sterling Publishing Company, is recommended.

There are, however, many frame designs made without the router. There are also a variety of ways of modifying the designs to form rabbeted lips for positioning the photos. For example, two layers of thin wood with different sized photo openings can be glued face to face. *See Photo No. 13.*

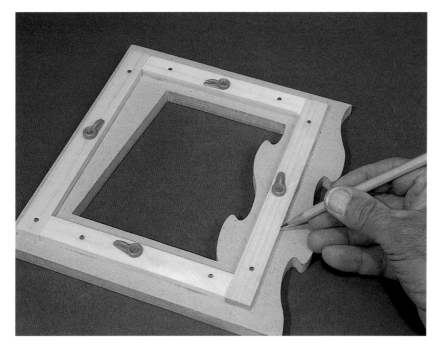

Photo No. 13. MDF frame material with strips nailed to the back side to form a rabbet-like lip for the photo. Note the use of turn buttons to keep the photo and backer in place.

Safety

The process of using and understanding any power tool will contribute to the success and sense of accomplishment that come with a job well done. The materials used by a crafts-person can be dangerous and potentially lethal.

The combination of potentially noxious dust, harmful chemicals and paints, high noise levels, sharp tools, and high quantities of electricity make it imperative that the crafts-person operates a safe, clean, and well thought-out environment. The risk of injury should never be underestimated.

Remember the following safety guidelines:
- Understand and observe strict rules with regard to manufacturer's instructions in the safe operation of all tools.
- Always wear a respirator or dust mask while working.
- Wear eye and ear protection when working with power tools.
- Never allow fingers to come near any moving blades or cutters.
- Wear appropriate attire – a heavy work apron, no jewelry, and no loose sleeves or ties.
- Wear appropriate footwear to protect feet from sharp or dropped objects.
- Feel comfortable when using power tools. Think out your project in its entirety and understand all

aspects of it before beginning.

- Always keep your mind on your work. Do not allow your mind to wander or be distracted when using power tools or sharp objects.

Above all, never work when tired, in a hurry, or not in the mood. Put the project down for today and come back to it later, in a better frame of mind and with time to spare. Use common sense at all times and each and every new challenging project or idea will be equally satisfying.

Tips: Usually, it is safest to cut out the inside opening and rout the rabbet immediately thereafter. Do this before working the wood with delicate, piercing scroll cuts or cutting the outside profile, which usually makes the work piece smaller and more dangerous to rout.

Rabbeting

A number of alternate rabbeting techniques are shown in *Photos No. 13–15 and No. 16–18 on page 18.*

Sometimes these techniques can be interchanged to provide rabbets on different patterns. Many of the router rabbeting techniques can be

Photo No. 14. Strips of purchased wood known as screen mouldings are overlaid to the front surface of this Baltic birch frame. They overlap the opening to create a rabbet all around. Notice the various shapes of screen mouldings available.

Photo No. 15. A ¾"-thick piece of solid butternut with a painted ⅛" overlay. The overlay is cut so that it has a smaller opening than the butternut frame, creating a nice rabbet.

Photo No. 16. A delicate frame cut from ¼" solid paduk. Note how the backer, with larger cut opening than the front, creates a rabbet all around.

Photo No. 17. Routed rabbet in MDF with a special ball bearing pilot that guides the bit around the inside opening.

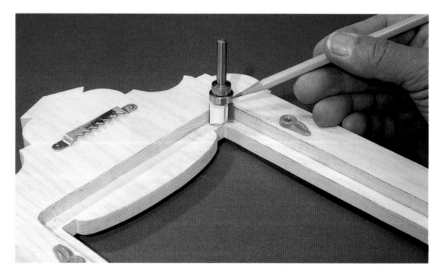

Photo No. 18. A straight, general purpose router bit was used to cut this rabbet of varying width. This bit was guided by a top (shank mounted) bearing following a straight edge. Multiple passes were required to rout away the full curved top edge shown. Note the saw-tooth picture hanger.

eliminated by attaching another layer to the back with a larger sawn opening. *See Photos No. 15 on page 17, No. 16, and No. 25 on page 21.*

Decorative & Functional Overlays

Gluing scroll-sawn ornamentation onto the face of frames creates an interesting look. *See Photos No. 19–21 and No. 22 on page 20.* Overlays are generally sawn from thin plywoods or thin solid woods, generally ⅛" or less. Gluing overlays onto frames that are to be coated with a stained or natural finish requires some careful work. Avoid smearing wood glue and watch for excess squeeze-out, as it will create a discolored blotch in the finish. The best fastening technique is accomplished by strategically placing droplets of wood glue. Instant or super glue is also recommended.

Photo No. 15 on page 17 shows an interesting frame overlay design. Painted ⅛" plywood, with its opening sawn smaller than

Photo No. 20. Here, the MDF frame is paired with a hardwood frame with a thin overlay and routed edges.

Photo No. 19. MDF frame with routed edges and glued ⅛" plywood overlay.

Photo No. 21. Mahogany with ⅛" solid mahogany overlays glued in place with small droplets of wood glue or instant adhesive. Notice the beveled chamfer cut routed around the opening.

Photo No. 22. Softening the sharp edges from delicate overlays is more safely done after being glued in place. Here, a flutter wheel is being used.

Photo No. 23. This ¼" thick frame is too thin to have rabbeted lips. Here, thumb tacks hold the photo with cardboard backer to the thin frame.

that of the thicker butternut backer, creates the rabbet for the photo.

Mounting Photos

Mounting the photos into the frames can be done by a variety of methods. If the frame stock is very thin, such as the ¹⁄₁₆"-thick plywood and sheet magnet frames, simply scissor-cut it to a size that overlaps the opening and tape it on. Or, use thumb tacks as shown in *Photo No. 23*.

Small nails, with a cardboard backer, work well for thicker frames. *Photo No. 24* shows a hinged door which acts as a backer. Typically, inexpensive turn buttons as shown in *Photos No. 13 on page 16, No. 16 on page 18, No. 18 on page 18, and No. 25* neatly hold the photo with a cardboard backer (or two) in place.

Finishing

As mentioned earlier, personal preference should be the determining factor when choosing how to finish and decorate the frames.

To finish fine hardwoods and beautifully figured woods so their natural colors and distinguishing characteristics are featured:

- Avoid high-gloss surface coatings. Gloss finishes highlight poor workmanship, such as insufficient sanding, mill marks, glue spots, stain blotches, scratches, and uneven surfaces. *See Photos No. 20 and No. 21 on page 19, and No. 22–27.*
- Use a penetrating rather than surface finish like a varnish. Danish oil is a good choice and is best applied with a dip-flooding process in a shallow pan. *See Photo No. 27.*

Photo No. 26. Pine used with purchased toy wheels create this novel frame that can be left unfinished or given a coat of clear sealer.

Photo No. 24. Small brads hold the cardboard or plywood backer against the photo.

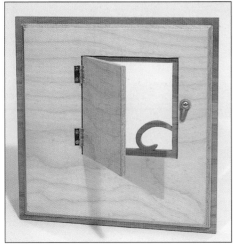

Photo No. 25. Here, a hinged door, carefully sawn from the plywood backer, holds the photo in place.

Photo No. 27. Dip-flooding ornate fretwork with penetrating oil in a shallow pan is an easy finishing technique.

Finish inexpensive plywoods by experimenting with staining and painting techniques:

- Apply watercolor paint to frames. Use one color to yield a staining effect, as shown on the upper right corner of the frame. Combine colors and values to create more depth and interest, as on the lower right corner of the frame. To confine paint to a specific area of the frame, as on the lower left corner of the frame, cut into wood with a craft knife to define the area and prevent colors from running. The upper left corner shows a bit of sparkle added to the frame. First, coat the painted area with découpage medium. Then, sprinkle clear glitter over the wet surface. Allow to dry. *See Photo No. 28.*

- Base-coat the entire surface wtih one color of acrylic paint. Cover the area with two to three smooth, even coats of paint. *See Photo No. 29.*

- Apply a wash finish to the frame by mixing one part acrylic paint and three parts water and brushing several even coats of light wash (allowing each coat to dry thoroughly) to produce a soft, but deep, transparent color. *See Photo No. 30.*

- Paint the frame with a dark color of acrylic paint. Create texture with a lighter shade of paint and a stiff brush. *See Photo No. 31.*

- Create a mottled finish, using several different colors of acrylic paint and a sponge or stencil brush. Load sponge or brush with just a bit of one color of paint. Bounce the sponge or brush on a paper towel to remove excess paint and then apply paint lightly to the frame. Repeat with remaining color(s). Vary dot sizes to create shadow and texture. *See Photo No. 32.*

Photo No. 28. This frame has been finished using four different staining and painting techniques to demonstrate how a finish can transform the wood piece.

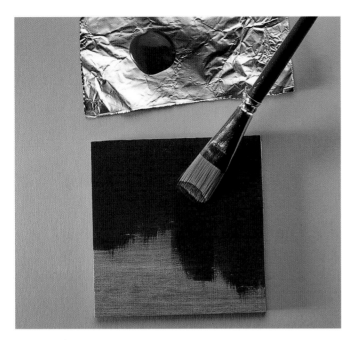

Photo No. 29. Base-coat the frame with two to three smooth, even coats of acrylic paint. For the Daisy frame project found on page 95, contrasting colors of paint are applied to the individual pieces of the frame .

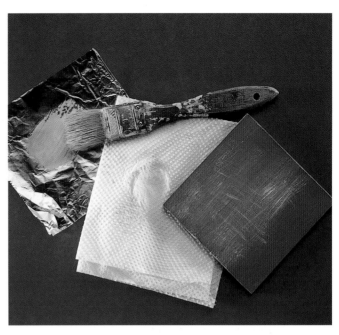

Photo No. 31. Add texture to the frame with a dry-brush technique. For the Record frame project found on page 62, a black frame was dry-brushed with gray acrylic paint to simulate the grooves of a record .

Photo No. 30. Combine water and acrylic paint to produce a color wash. Brush several even coats over the frame, allowing each coat to dry. The Sailboat frame project found on page 77 combines two color washes—one on the frame and one on the overlay.

Photo No. 32. The Corner Leaf frame project found on page 31 shows a mottled effect that is created with a sponging or stippling technique. Load a sponge or stencil brush with one color of acrylic paint. Remove excess paint and lightly apply to the frame.

- Novelty paints, available in craft stores, such as aerosol sprays, produce stone, marble, antique crackle, and other unusual finishes almost instantly. *See Photo No. 33.*
- Follow manufacturer's instructions to apply gold leafing over a dark color of acrylic paint on a frame. The result is a rich, dramatic finish. *See Photo No. 34.*
- Apply paper or fabric to a frame with découpage medium. Brush découpage medium onto back of paper or fabric. Place onto frame as desired. Press out any air bubbles. Brush several light coats of medium over paper or fabric, allowing medium to dry between coats. *See Photo No. 35.*

Photo No. 34. Gold leaf is an easy way to give a rich look to an inexpensive plywood. (Lucky Star frame project instructions are found on page 50.)

Photo No. 33. Some unusual finishes come direct from handy aerosol cans. They are usually available in various colors and create an almost instant appearance. (Granite frame project instructions are found on page 42.)

Photo No. 35. The lines of music on this paper define the theme of the frame (Music frame project instructions found on page 34). The paper was wrinkled and then applied to the wooden frame with découpage medium.

Stands & Hangers

Frames that are ½" or more in thickness can be made to stand with the support of a single wooden dowel. *See Photo No. 36.*

Simply drill a ¼"-diameter hole half-way into the thickness of the stock, centered and near the lower edge of the frame. Depending on the design or style of the frame, the hole may need to be slightly angled. Plan to obtain the best viewing angle for the front side of the frame.

Cut a dowel a few inches longer than anticipated. Then, through trial and error, gradually shorten the dowel length until the frame is supported as desired. If desired, glue the dowel into the frame.

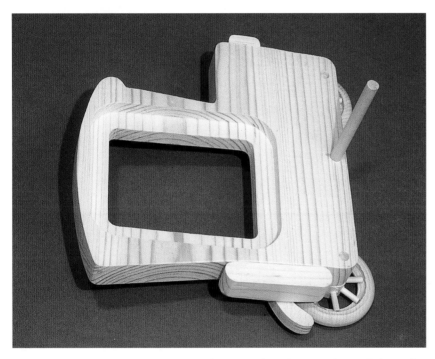

Photo No. 36. Here is an example of a short dowel inserted at a slight angle, which provides the support for standing frames.

There are numerous types of hangers, designed to be mounted onto the back of the frame, that are readily available at hardware stores. These include sawtooth hangers, which serve to compensate for mounting errors so that the frame will hang straight on the wall. The standard sawtooth hanger is attached with small mounting nails while the self-fastening sawtooth hanger does not require any nails—just tap it into the wood. The standard picture hanger has a flat round opening that can be set onto a nail in the wall. The triangle hanger has a swinging head that adjusts the angle of the frame so it lies fairly flat against the wall.

Decorating Tips

Once the frame is complete, take just a moment to contemplate the manner in which it will be displayed.

First, consider the foundation for the frame. It can sit upon a traditional surface, such as a bookshelf, a hutch, or an individual shelf strip. Perhaps it would lend itself to a more novel setting such, as on a foot locker or attached to a folding screen. With a bit of ribbon, the frame may even be hung from a bulletin board, a hat rack, or a wreath.

Next, choose accents to complement the frame and its foundation. Tradtional accents are candle holders, flowers, plants, ornamental pieces, and vases. Antiques, baskets, birds' nests, bowls, clocks, clothing, and sports equipment are more trendy accents. For a personal accent, use treasures such as books, toys, trophies, or other objects that hold special meaning or sentimental value.

Picture Frames

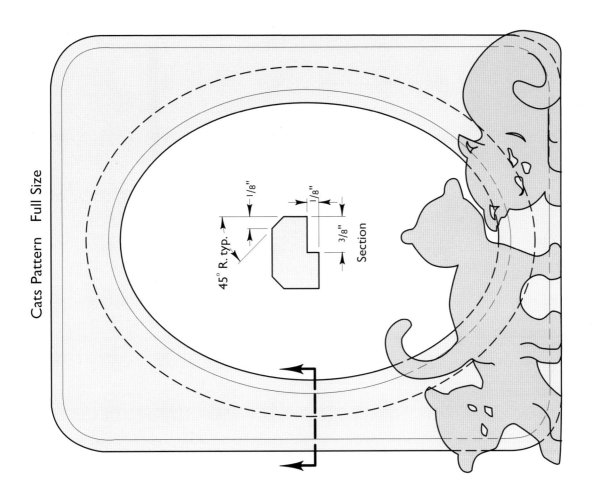

45° R. typ.

1/8"

1/8"

3/8"

Section

Cats
materials:
cardboard for backer
hardwood – ½" x 5½" x 7¼"
instant adhesive or wood glue
plywood for overlay – ¹⁄₁₆" or ⅛" x 2¾" x 4¼"
router

instructions:
1. Make two photocopies of pattern. Adhere one copy to each wood piece. Cut out profiles and openings.

2. Rabbet inside edge of frame with router. *See Photos No. 17 and No. 18 on page 18.*

3. Chamfer inside and outside edges of frame with router.

4. Glue overlay onto frame.

5. Finish as desired.

6. Cut oval cardboard backer approximately 4⅜" x 5⅜".

Bears Pattern   Full Size

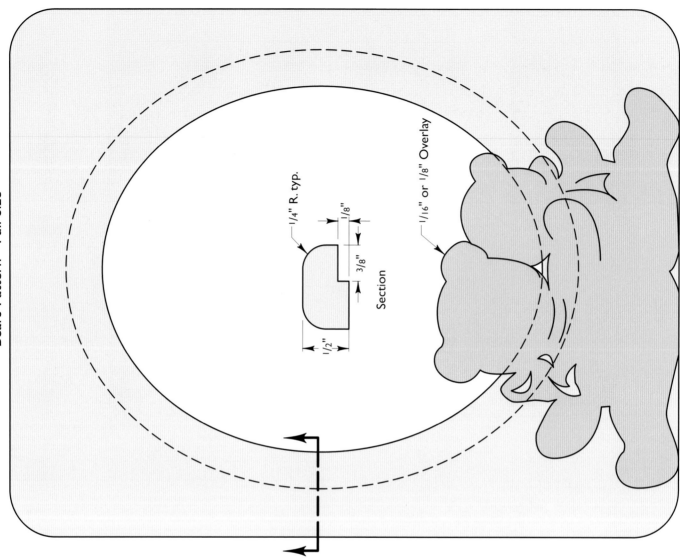

¼" R. typ.

⅛"

3⁄8"

½"

Section

1⁄16" or ⅛" Overlay

Bears

materials:
cardboard for backer
hardwood – ½" x 4¼" x 5½"
instant adhesive or wood glue
plywood for overlay – ⅛" x 4½" x 2"
router

instructions:
1. Make two photocopies of pattern. Adhere one copy to each wood piece. Cut out profiles and openings.

2. Rabbet inside edge of frame with router. *See Photos No. 17 and No. 18 on page 18.*

3. Round-over inside and outside edges of frame with router.

4. Glue overlay onto frame.

5. Finish as desired.

6. Cut oval cardboard backer approximately 3⅝" x 4⅝".

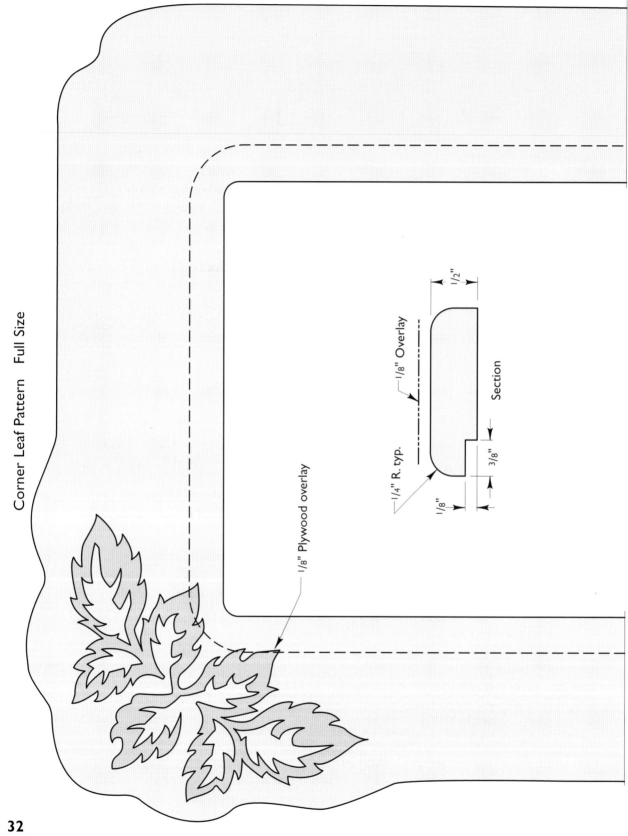

Corner Leaf Pattern   Full Size

$1/8$" Plywood overlay

$1/8$" Overlay

$1/4$" R. typ.

$1/8$"

$3/8$"

$1/2$"

Section

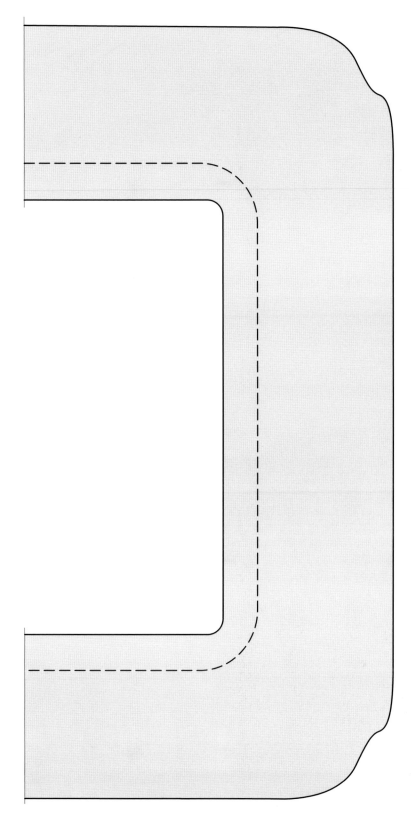

Corner Leaf

materials:
birch plywood or solid stock for
    overlay — $\frac{1}{8}$" x $2\frac{1}{8}$" x $3\frac{7}{8}$"
cardboard for backer
fine hardwood, MDF, pine, or ply-
    wood — $\frac{1}{2}$" x $8\frac{1}{2}$" x $10\frac{1}{2}$"
instant adhesive or wood glue
router

instructions:
1. Make two photocopies of
pattern. Adhere one copy to each
wood piece. Cut out profiles and
openings.

2. Rabbet inside edge of frame with
router. *See Photos No. 17 and No. 18
on page 18.*

3. Round-over outside and inside
edges of frame $\frac{1}{4}$" radius with
router.

4. Glue overlay onto frame either
before or after finishing—whichever
is most appropriate for type of
finish used.

5. Cut cardboard backer approximately $5\frac{1}{8}$" x $6\frac{3}{4}$".

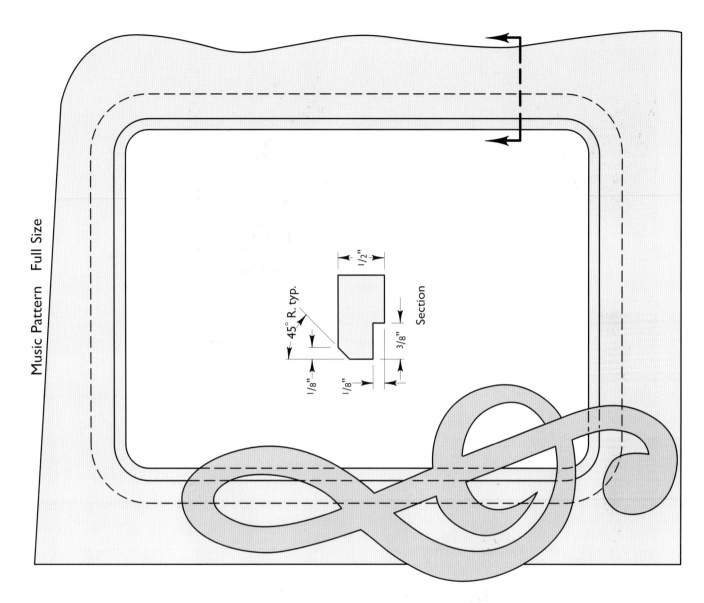

Music Pattern Full Size

45° R. typ.

½"

Section

3/8"

⅛"

⅛"

Music

materials:

cardboard for backer

instant adhesive or wood glue

MDF, pine, or plywood – ½" x 5⅝" x 7"

plywood or solid wood for overlay – ⅛" or
   ¼" x 2" x 5½"

router

instructions:

1. Make two photocopies of pattern. Adhere one copy to each wood piece. Cut out profiles and openings.

2. Rabbet inside edge of frame with router. *See Photos No. 17 and No. 18 on page 18.*

3. Chamfer inside edge of frame with router.

4. Glue overlay onto frame either before or after finishing—whichever is most appropriate for type of finish used.

5. Cut cardboard backer approximately 4¼" x 5⅝".

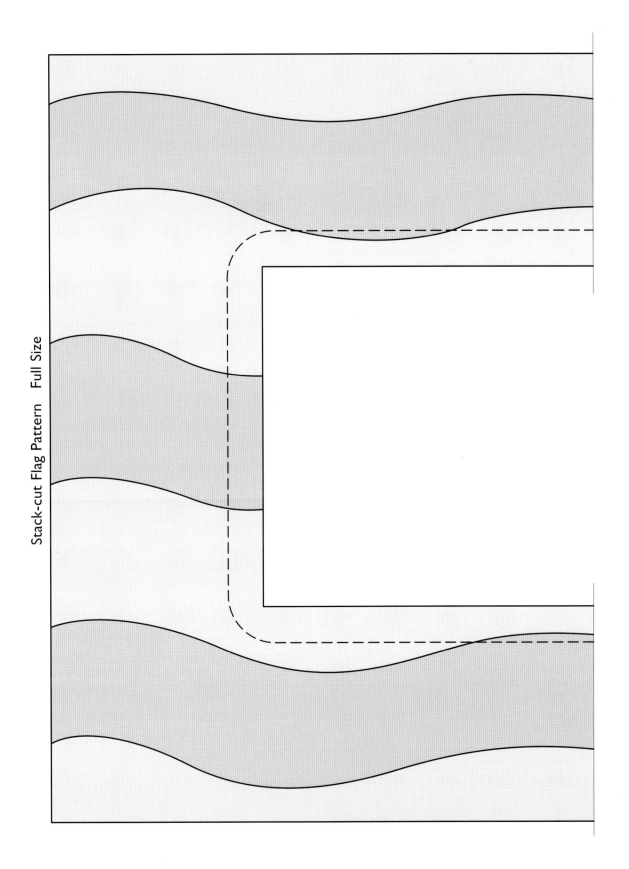

Stack-cut Flag Pattern   Full Size

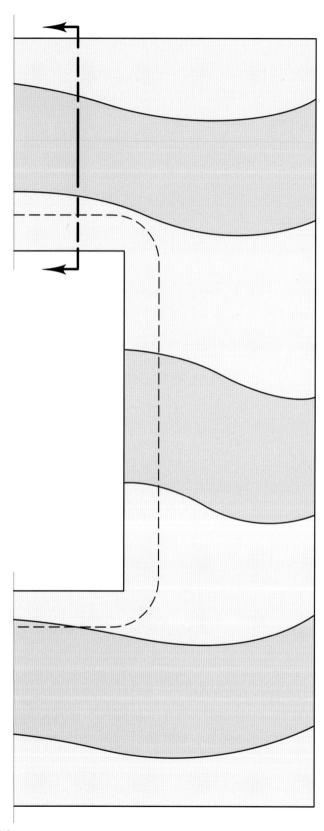

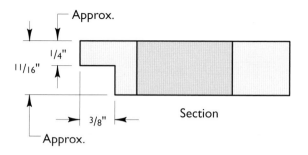

Tips: *Select woods for best natural color contrast and similar hardness. Some combinations are: walnut and ash (as shown in photos), walnut and maple, cherry and maple, oak and maple, or other hardwoods. Softwood combinations include: butternut and pine, cedar and basswood, redwood and pine, mahogany and pine.*

Stack-cut Flag

materials:
contrasting color woods of like density – ¾" x
    8" x 9⅛" (2)
instant adhesive or wood glue
router
sandpaper (100–150 grit)
table saw

instructions:
1. Prepare boards to size with an extra ½" in rough length.

2. Photocopy pattern. Adhere copy to top wood piece and secure both pieces together for stack-cutting. *See Photo No. SCF-1.*

3. Make certain the blade is sharp and the saw table is square to the blade.

4. Test blade sharpness on scrap or waste area of inside opening of stacked pieces.

5. Cut stack into strips as shown in *Photo No. SCF-1.*

6. Glue strips together into single panel with interchanging colors.

7. Surface or sand both sides as necessary and trim ends even on table saw.

8. Layout inside opening (2¼" in from all edges).

9. Cut out inside opening of each frame.

10. Rabbet openings with a router. *See Photo No. SCF-2.*

11. Sand and finish as desired.

12. Cut cardboard backer approximately 4" x 5⅛".

13. If desired, attach a simple stand to the back of frames. *See Photo No. SCF-2. Refer to Stands & Hangers in the General Instructions on page 25.*

Tips: *Stack-cutting (sawing one or more pieces on top of each other) is a basic scrolling technique employed to make identical pieces. This technique was applied here to make these two similar-looking frames, each with identically sawn components, at the same time.*

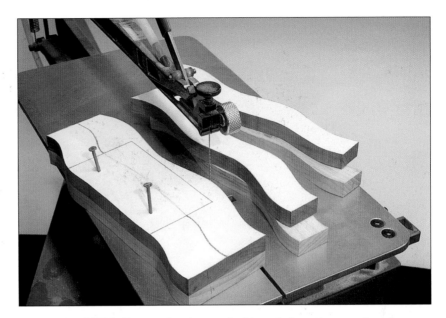

Photo No. SCF-1. Pieces of walnut and white ash (or other species of choice) are held together (nailed in the waste area) and stack-cut, producing two identical pieces of each component. These are used to create two separate frames. The layers are interchanged and glued together with other pieces to create alternating colors of wood. The result is actually two individual frame blanks—each with contrasting stripes.

Photo No. SCF-2. A rear view shows the two frames with the router-cut rabbeted edge around the opening and dowels that support the frames.

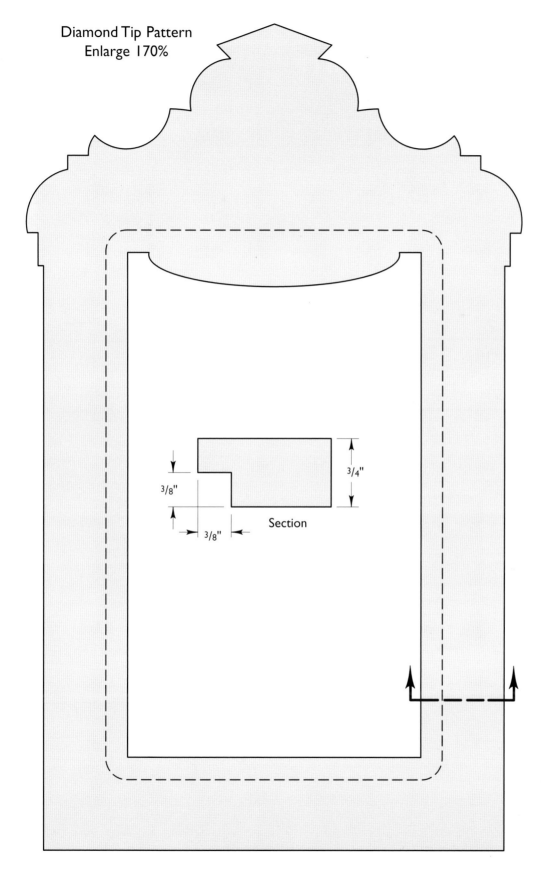

Diamond Tip Pattern
Enlarge 170%

3/4"

3/8"

3/8"

Section

Diamond Tip

materials:
cardboard for
    backer
instant adhesive or
    wood glue
molded appliqués
pine – ¾" x 9" x
    14⅝"
router
sandpaper (100–
    150 grit)

instructions:
1. Enlarge and
photocopy pattern.
Adhere pattern to
wood piece. Cut
out profile and
opening.

2. Rabbet inside
edge of frame with
router. *See Photos
No. 17 and No. 18
on page 18.*

3. Glue molded
appliqués to frame
as desired. Sand
and finish frame as
desired.

4. Cut cardboard
backer approx-
imately 5¾" x 9¼".

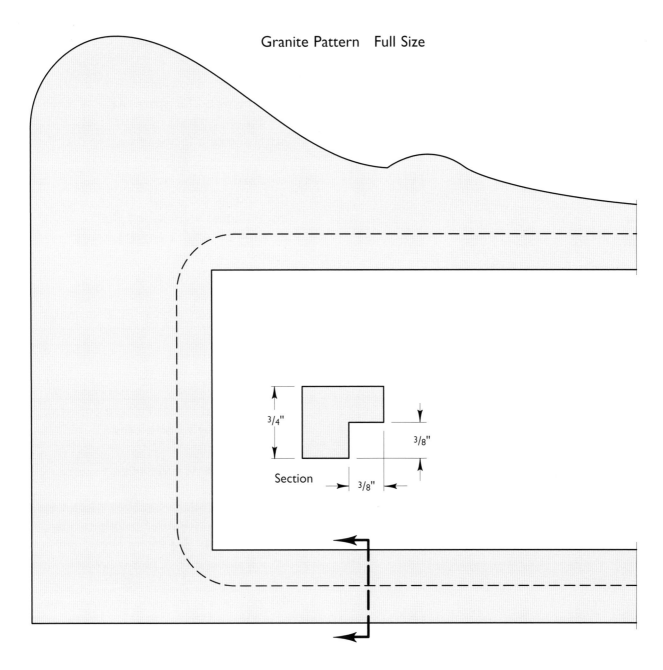

Granite Pattern   Full Size

3/4"

3/8"

Section   3/8"

Granite

materials:
cardboard for backer
MDF or pine – ¾" x 6¼" x 10"
router
sandpaper (100–150 grit)

instructions:
1. Photocopy pattern. Adhere copy to wood. Cut out profile and opening.

2. Rabbet inside edge of frame with router. *See Photos No. 17 and No. 18 on page 18.*

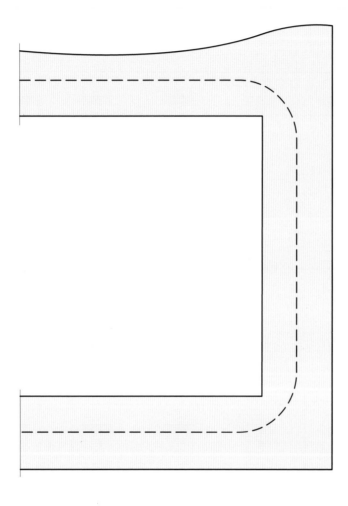

3. Sand and finish as desired.

4. Cut cardboard backer approximately 3⅝" x 8⅛".

Car (photo on page 46)
materials:
birch plywood for fender – ⅜" x 1¾" x 7¼"
birch plywood for spare tire – ¾" x ½" x 2⅜"
birch plywood for headlamp – ¾" x ¼" x ⅞"
cardboard for backer
drill and ⁷⁄₃₂" bit
instant adhesive or wood glue
pine for car – ¾" x 6⅛" x 6⅛"
router
sandpaper (60–150 grit)
scissors
wooden wheels with axles, 2" diameter (2)

instructions:
1. Photocopy pattern. Scissor-cut copy into individual pieces. Adhere copies to corresponding wood pieces.

2. Cut out picture opening.

3. For safety reasons, rabbet inside edge of opening with router before cutting outside profile. *See Photos No. 17 and No. 18 on page 18.* Cut out profiles.

4. Drill holes in frame to accommodate wheel axels.

5. Round-over edges of headlamp and spare tire, carefully sanding by hand.

6. Glue fenders, headlamp, spare tire, and wheels onto car.

7. Finish as desired.

8. Cut cardboard backer approximately 3¼" x 4".

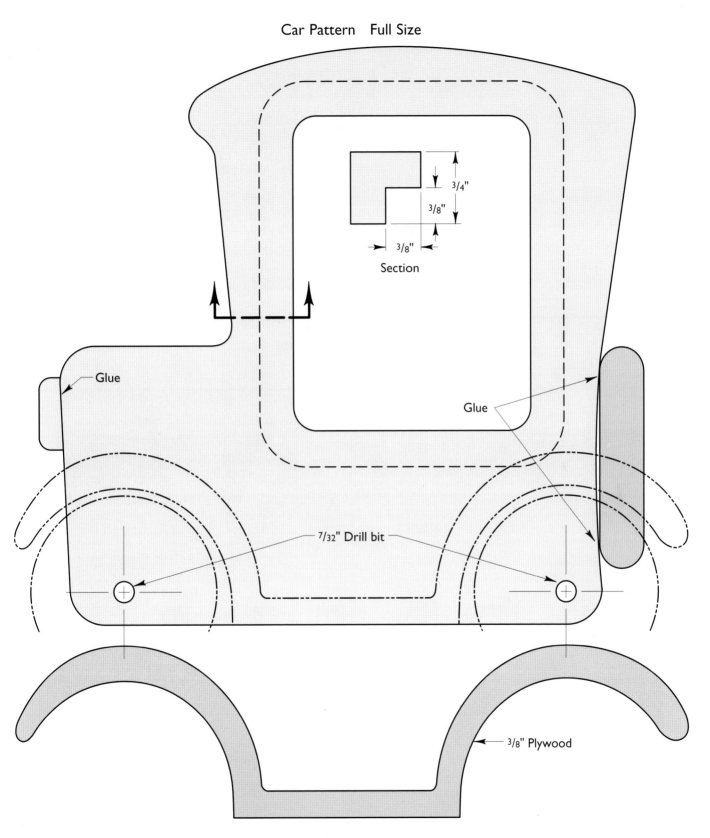

Car Pattern   Full Size

3/4"

3/8"

3/8"

Section

Glue

Glue

7/32" Drill bit

3/8" Plywood

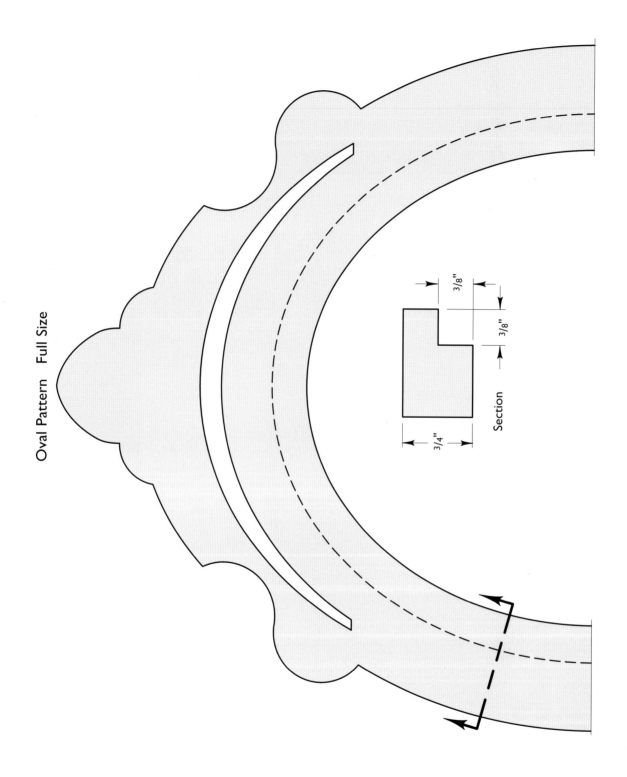

Oval Pattern   Full Size

3/8"

3/8"

Section

3/4"

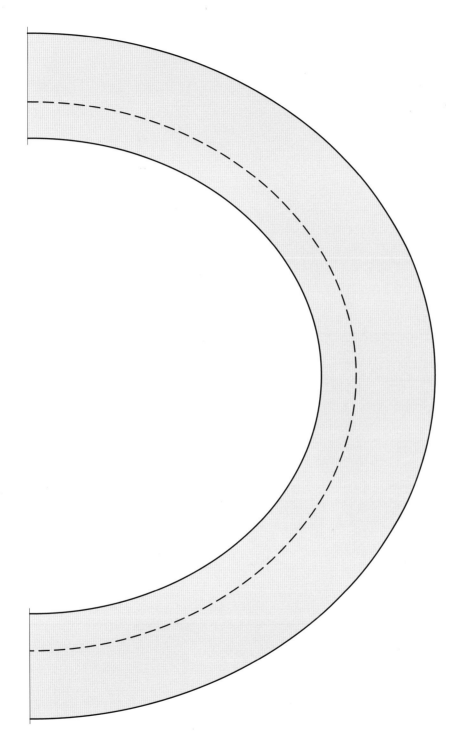

Oval

materials:
cardboard for backer
MDF or pine – ¾" x 7⅛" x
    10¼"
router
sandpaper (100–150 grit)

instructions:
1. Photocopy pattern. Adhere copy to wood. Cut out profile and openings.

2. Rabbet inside edge of frame with router. *See Photos No. 17 and No. 18 on page 18.*

3. Sand and finish as desired.

4. Cut oval cardboard backer approximately 5½" x 6⅞".

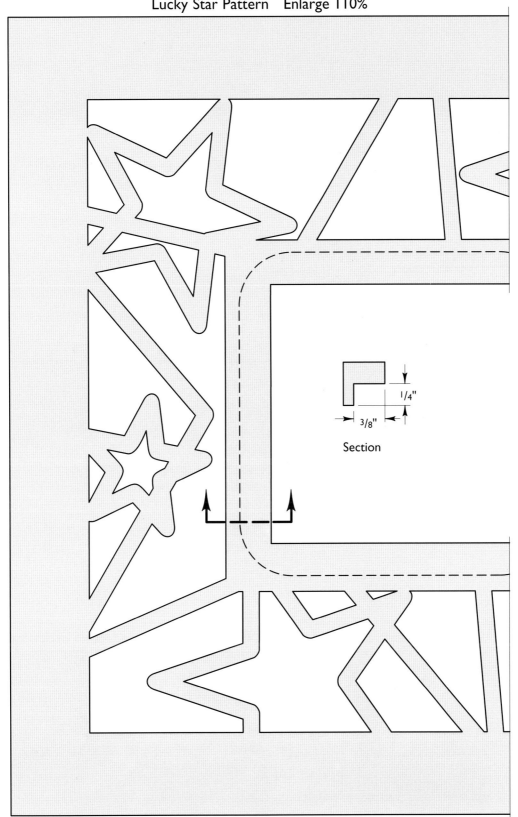

Section

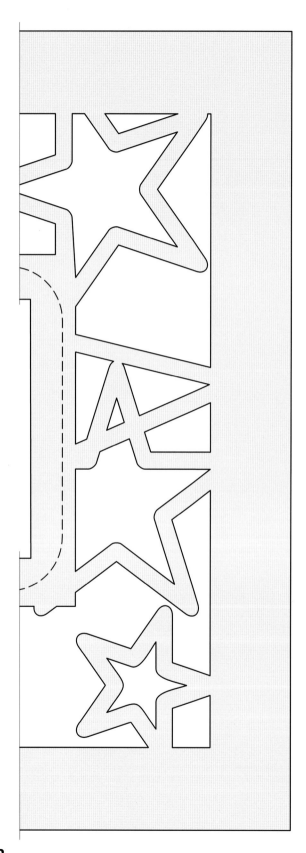

Lucky Star
materials:
cardboard for backer
MDF, plywood, or solid wood – ½" x 8¾" x 8¾"
router
sandpaper (100–150 grit)

instructions:
1. Enlarge and photocopy pattern. Adhere copy to wood. Cut out profile and openings.

2. Rabbet inside edge of frame with router. *See Photos No. 17 and No. 18 on page 18.*

3. Sand and finish as desired.

4. Cut cardboard backer approximately 3½" x 3½".

Lacy Oval (photo on page 54)
materials:
baltic birch plywood – ⅜" or ½" x 10½" x 13½"
cardboard for backer
router
sandpaper (100–150 grit)

instructions:
1. Enlarge and photocopy pattern. Adhere copy to wood piece. Cut out profile and openings.

2. Rabbet inside edge of frame with router. *See Photos No. 17 and No. 18 on page 18.*

3. Sand and finish as desired.

4. Cut oval cardboard backer approximately 5⅛" x 7¼".

Lacy Oval Pattern   Enlarge 165%

1/8"

3/8"

3/8"

Section

Double Hinge Pattern   Enlarge 120%

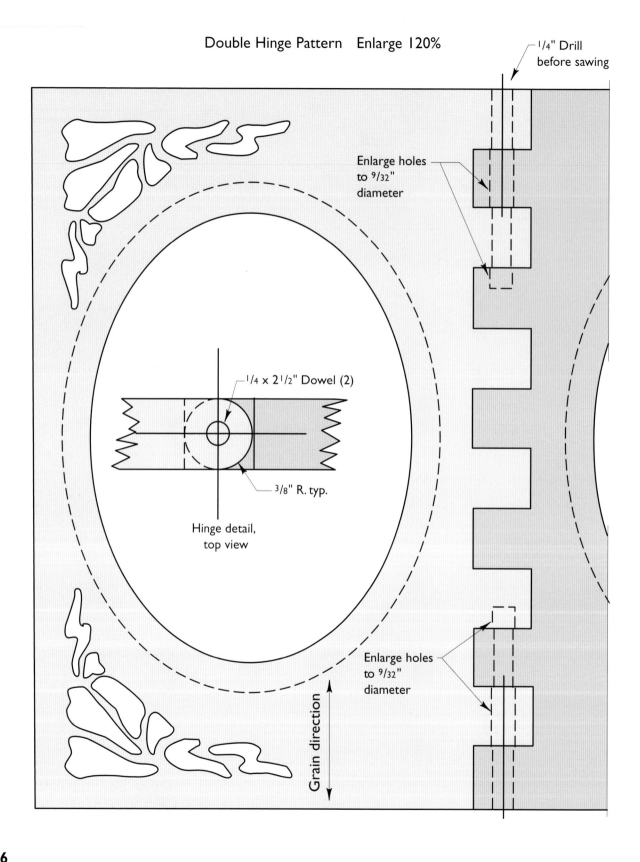

¹/₄" Drill
before sawing

Enlarge holes
to ⁹/₃₂"
diameter

¹/₄ x 2¹/₂" Dowel (2)

³/₈" R. typ.

Hinge detail,
top view

Enlarge holes
to ⁹/₃₂"
diameter

Grain direction

56

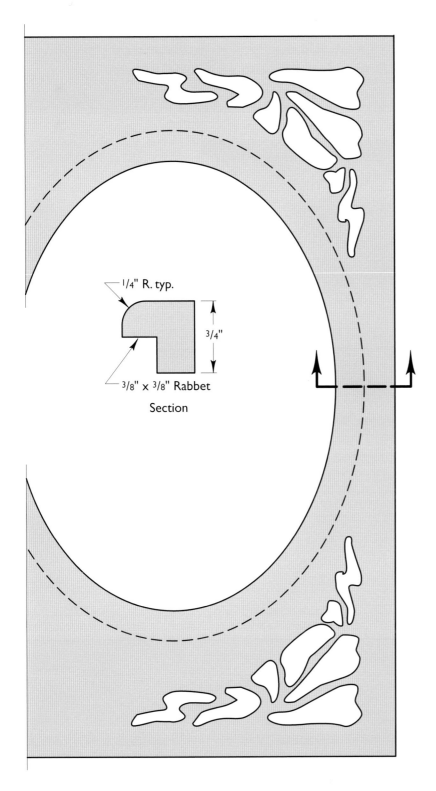

1/4" R. typ.

3/4"

3/8" x 3/8" Rabbet

Section

Tips: *This frame is made from one piece of wood that is drilled and cut to create its hinge. It is almost impossible to drill one perfectly centered and aligned hole continuously from top to bottom. The central area of the hinge is actually nonfunctional.*

All that is necessary is to drill part way into each of the second fingers from the top and the same from the bottom. No one will ever know that the hinge is not pinned all the way through unless given an up-close inspection.

Double Hinge

materials:
awl
brads
cardboard for backers
dowels – ¼" diameter,
    approximately 2¼" long (2)
drill and ¼" bit
router and ⅜" bit
softwood – ¾" x 12¼" x 9"
wax

instructions:
1. Enlarge and photocopy pattern. Adhere copy to wood piece. Cut out profile.

2. Transfer the vertical center of the hinge fingers to the top and bottom edges of the wood piece.

3. Mark center starting points for drilling hole at top and bottom with awl.

4. Carefully drill pin holes precisely at right angles as deep as possible, using a v-block drilling guide. *See Photo No. DH-1.* (A self-centering doweling jig may also be used.)

5. Square the saw table to the blade. Cut the hinge fingers, tensioning more than usual. *See Photo No. DH-2.*

6. Separate the two frames. Enlarge the pin holes in the appropriate fingers to ⁹⁄₃₂".

7. Cut out openings.

8. Round-over pin edges with router. *See Photo No. DH-3.* Rabbet and round-over inside edges of frame with router. *See Photos No. 17 and No. 18 on page 18.*

9. Cut dowels to equal depth of pin holes. Sand dowels as necessary to fit. Insert dowels and check hinging action.

10. Remove dowels, wax them, and insert them again. Drive a small brad into each dowel from the back.

11. Cut oval cardboard backer approximately 4¼" x 5½".

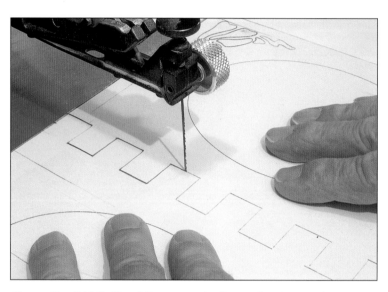

Photo No. DH-2. Carefully cut on the line and make consistent right angle turns as shown.

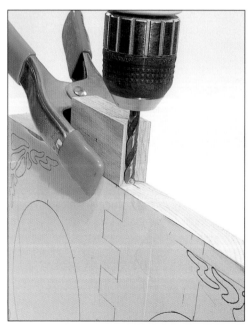

Photo No.DH-1. Drilling for the dowel hinge pin is done before sawing the square hinge fingers to separate the two frames. A shop made v-block helps to guide the bit.

Photo No. DH-3. Use a router table with a fence and a ⅜" round-over bit to shape the hinge side edges.

CORNER SCROLL

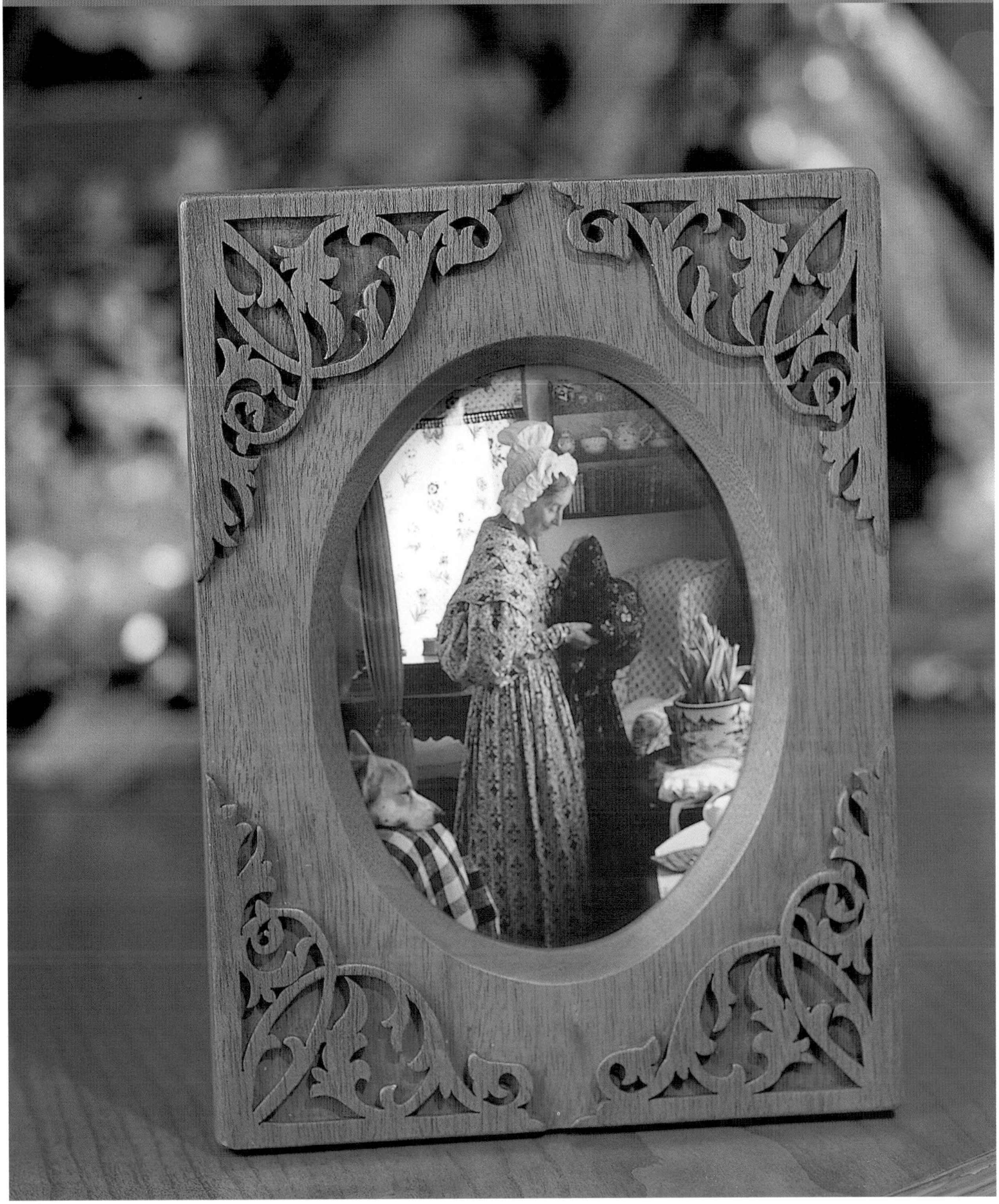

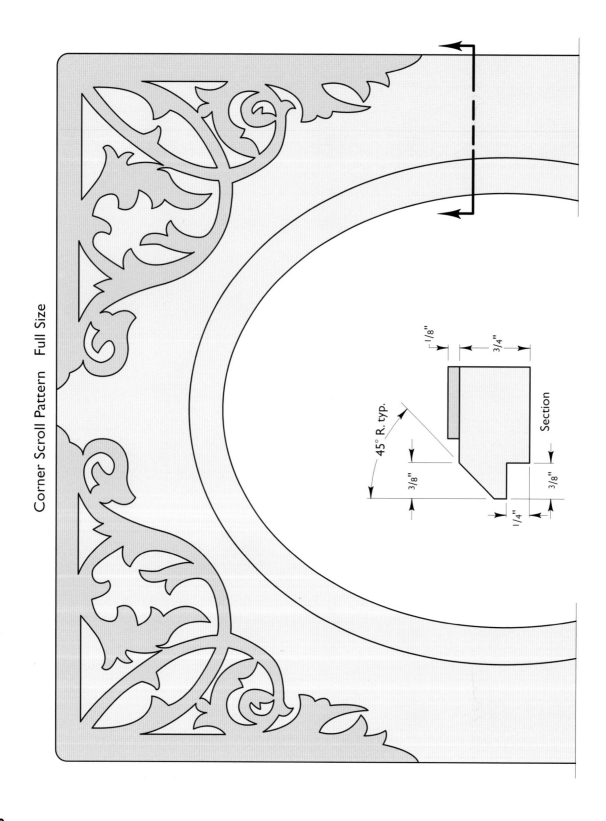

Corner Scroll Pattern   Full Size

1/8"

3/4"

45° R. typ.

3/8"

Section

3/8"

1/4"

Corner Scroll

materials:
cardboard for backer
hardwood – ¾" x 7⅜" x 9¾"
hardwood for overlays – ⅛" x
    3⅝" x 4" (4)
instant adhesive or wood glue
sandpaper (60–150 grit)
router

instructions:
1. Photocopy pattern. Adhere copy to wood piece. Cut out frame profile and opening.

2. Rabbet inside edge of frame with router. *See Photos No. 17 and No. 18 on page 18.*

3. Chamfer inside and outside edges of frame with router.

4. Stack-cut overlay profile and openings, either two at a time or all four at once.

5. Sand all wood pieces—taking extra care with short grains on solid wood overlays.

6. Glue overlays onto frame. *See Photo No. 21 page 19.*

7. Sand edges and corners flush.

8. Finish as desired.

9. Cut oval cardboard backer approximately 5¼" x 6¾".

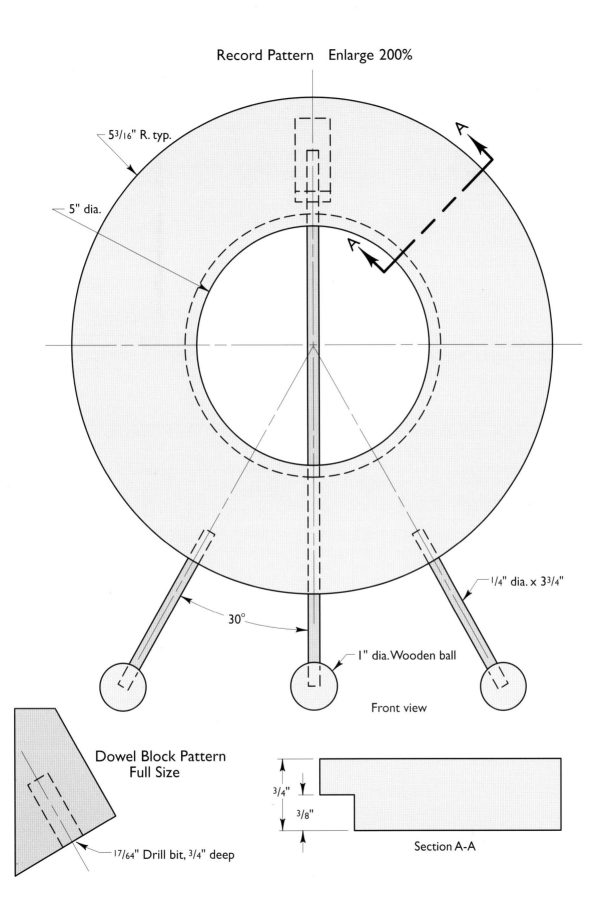

Record Pattern   Enlarge 200%

5³/₁₆" R. typ.

5" dia.

A

A

¹/₄" dia. x 3³/₄"

30°

I" dia. Wooden ball

Front view

Dowel Block Pattern
Full Size

¹⁷/₆₄" Drill bit, ³/₄" deep

³/₄"

³/₈"

Section A-A

Record

materials:

dowels – ¼" diameter, 3¾" long (2); ¼" diameter, 11" long

cardboard for backer

clamps

drill or drill press and ¹⁷⁄₆₄" bit

instant adhesive or wood glue

MDF, pine, or plywood – ¾" x 10⅜" diameter

power drum or disc sander

predrilled hardwood balls – 1" diameter (3)

router

sandpaper (100–150 grit)

instructions:

1. Directly layout circular frame with a compass or enlarge and photocopy pattern. Adhere copy to wood piece.

2. Rabbet inside edge of frame with router. *See Photos No. 17 and No. 18 on page 18.*

3. Layout front dowel leg center lines on face of wood piece, emerging from the center.

4. Layout vertical center line on back surface.

5. Scroll-cut circular shapes. Fair out curves with power drum or disc sander.

6. Extend dowel center lines over edge.

7. Clamp wood piece vertically on drill press and drill dowel holes.

8. Make and drill rear dowel block and glue to rear of frame. *See Record Diagram.*

9. Glue balls to dowels and glue front dowels in place. *See Record Diagram.*

10. If desired, enlarge hole in rear dowel block to make rear leg removable.

11. Sand and finish as desired.

12. Cut cardboard backer approximately 5¾" diameter.

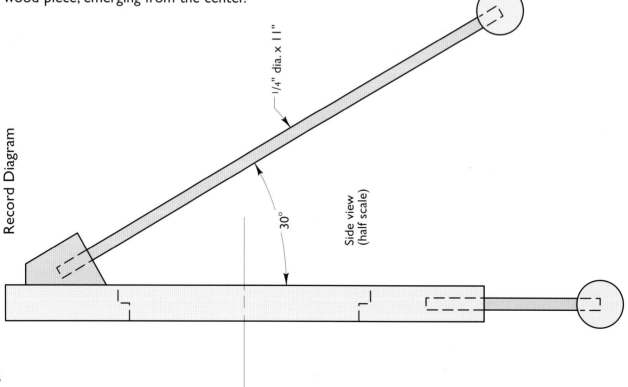

Record Diagram

¼" dia. x 11"

30°

Side view
(half scale)

WREATH

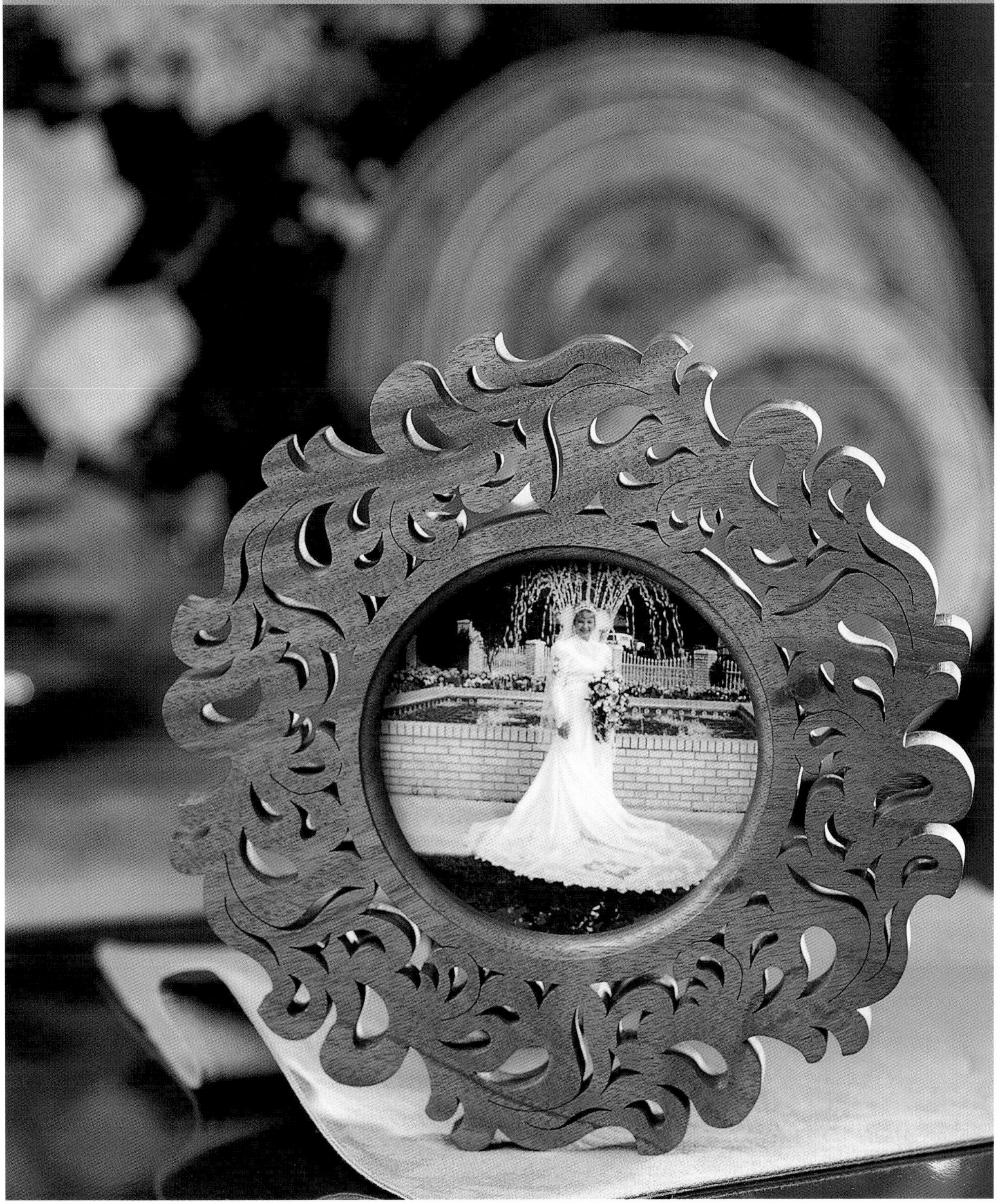

Wreath Pattern   Enlarge 120%

Rout bead, 1/4" R. typ.

3/4"

3/8"

3/8"

Section

Wreath

materials:
cardboard for backer
hardwood — ¾" x 10" x 10"
router
sandpaper (100–150 grit)

instructions:
1. Enlarge and photocopy pattern. Adhere copy to wood piece. Cut out profile and openings.

2. Rabbet inside edge with router. *See Photos No. 17 and No. 18 on page 18.*

3. Form a bead around inside edge with router.

4. Sand and finish as desired.

5. Cut cardboard backer approximately 5" in diameter.

Waves (photo on page 69)

materials:
cardboard for backer
instant adhesive or wood glue
MDF or plywood — ½" x 8⅞" x 9¼"
pine — ¼" x ¾" x 8¼" (2)
pine — ¼" x ¾" x 5⅞" (2)
sandpaper (100–150 grit)

instructions:
1. Photocopy pattern. Adhere copy to wood piece. Cut out profile and opening.

2. Following dotted lines, glue strips onto back of frame around opening, creating recess.

3. Sand and finish as desired.

4. Cut cardboard backer, approximately 5¾" x 6⅝".

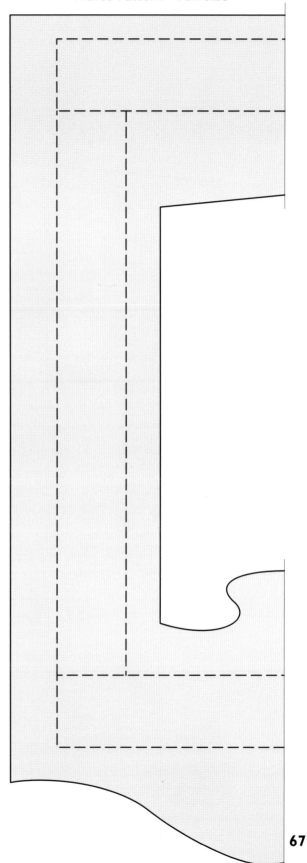

Waves Pattern   Full Size

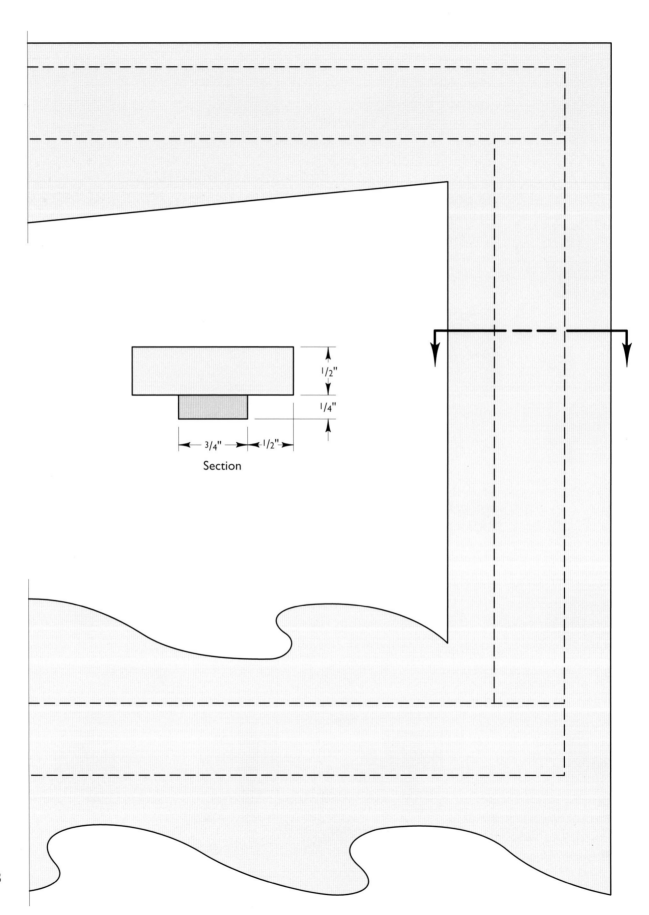

Section

1/2"

1/4"

3/4"   1/2"

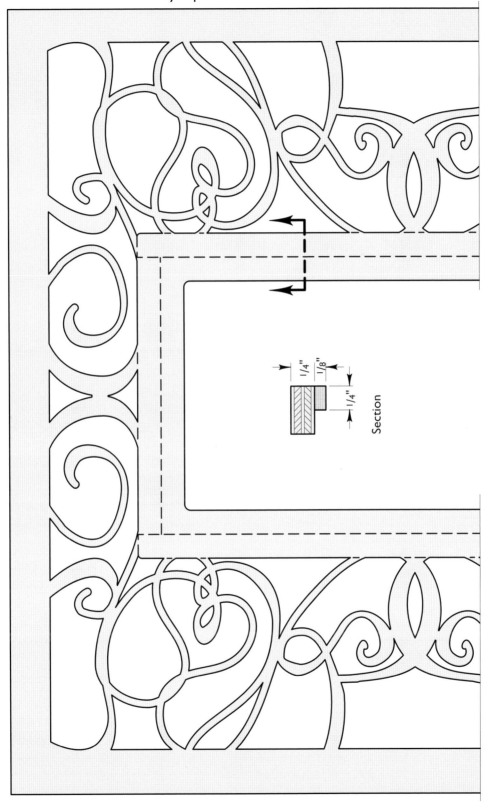

Section

1/4"   1/8"   1/4"

Lacy Square

materials:
baltic birch plywood – $\frac{1}{4}$" x $8\frac{3}{16}$" x $8\frac{3}{4}$"
baltic birch plywood – $\frac{1}{8}$" x $\frac{1}{4}$" x $5\frac{7}{8}$" (2)
baltic birch plywood – $\frac{1}{8}$" x $\frac{1}{4}$" x $2\frac{7}{8}$" (2)
cardboard for backer
instant adhesive or wood glue
sandpaper (100–150 grit)

instructions:
1. Photocopy pattern. Adhere copy to plywood. Cut out profile and openings.

2. Following dotted lines, glue strips onto back of frame around opening, creating recess.

3. Sand and finish as desired.

4. Cut cardboard backer approximately $2\frac{7}{8}$" x $5\frac{1}{4}$".

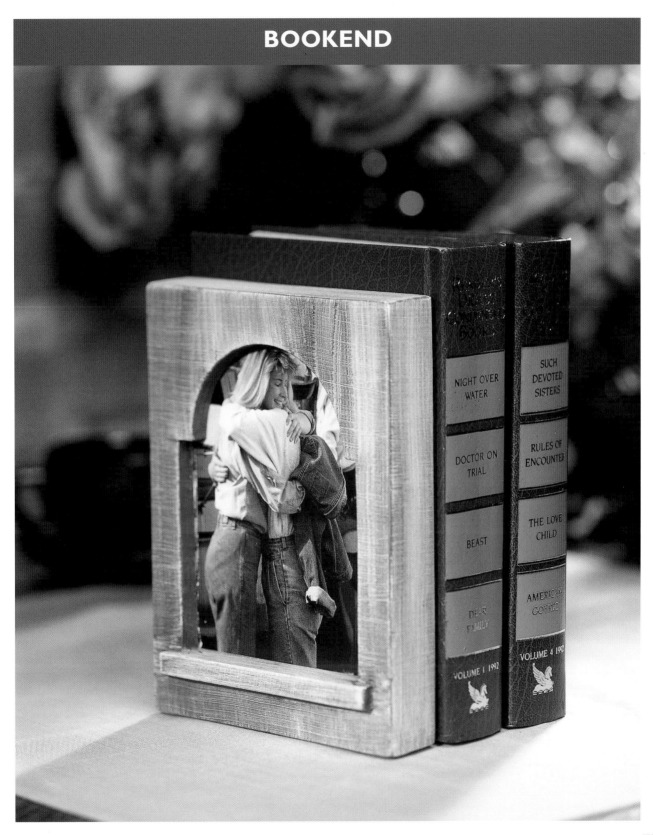

Bookend Pattern   Full Size

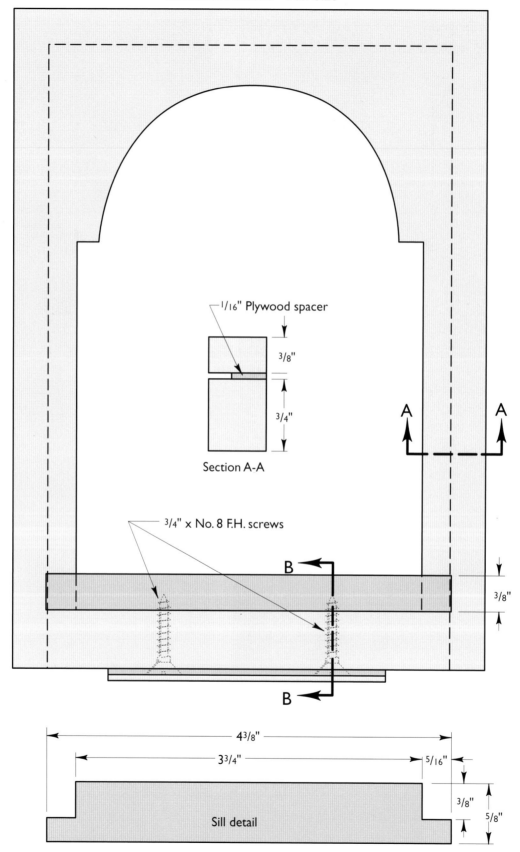

¹/₁₆" Plywood spacer

3/8"

3/4"

Section A-A

A   A

³/₄" x No. 8 F.H. screws

B

B

3/8"

4³/8"

3³/4"

⁵/₁₆"

3/8"

5/8"

Sill detail

Bookend Diagram

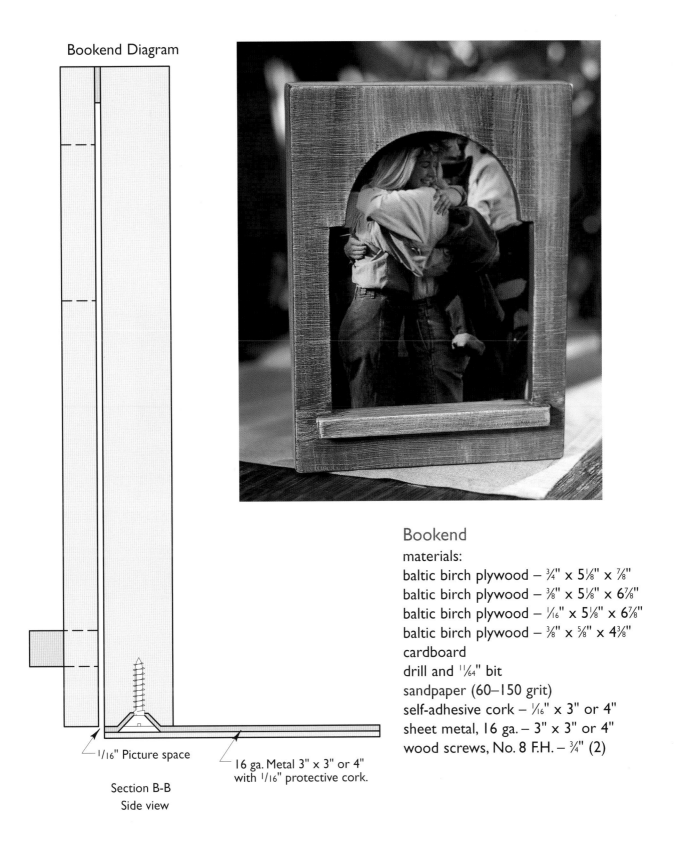

1/16" Picture space

Section B-B
Side view

16 ga. Metal 3" x 3" or 4"
with 1/16" protective cork.

Bookend
materials:
baltic birch plywood – ¾" x 5⅛" x ⅞"
baltic birch plywood – ⅜" x 5⅛" x 6⅞"
baltic birch plywood – 1/16" x 5⅛" x 6⅞"
baltic birch plywood – ⅜" x ⅝" x 4⅜"
cardboard
drill and 11/64" bit
sandpaper (60–150 grit)
self-adhesive cork – 1/16" x 3" or 4"
sheet metal, 16 ga. – 3" x 3" or 4"
wood screws, No. 8 F.H. – ¾" (2)

instructions:

1. Make two photocopies of patterns. Adhere copies to wood pieces. Cut out window, sill, and spacer. *See Photo No. BE-1.*

2. Glue and assemble layers. Remove any excess glue by slipping a piece of cardboard in and out of picture slot.

3. Sand outside edges flush and finish as desired.

4. Cut sheet metal to size, file edges and corners round and drill two $\frac{11}{64}$" screw holes.

5. Form sheet metal dimples to receive screw heads. *See Photos No. BE-2 and No. BE-3.*

6. Mark screw holes on bottom of wood. Drill $\frac{3}{32}$" pilot holes and countersink the holes excessively to allow dimpled sheet metal to fit.

7. Fasten sheet metal to bottom of frame.

8. Adhere protective cork to bottom of sheet metal. *See Photo No. BE-4.*

Photo No. BE-2. Dimple the sheet metal for flat head wood screws. Make a hardwood forming block with a $\frac{3}{16}$" hole deeply countersunk. Place a screw through the hole in the sheet metal and strike the screw head as necessary, using it as a form to dimple the metal.

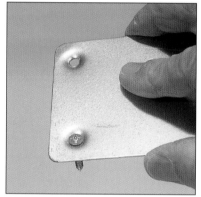

Photo No. BE-3. The completed metal plate with the dimpled metal around the holes allows the use of flat head screws to be flush to the bottom surface.

Photo No. BE-1. The wood components and the metal plate (with cork covering material).

Photo No. BE-4. After assembly, cover the bottom with $\frac{1}{16}$" self-adhesive cork or other protective material of your choice.

SAILBOAT

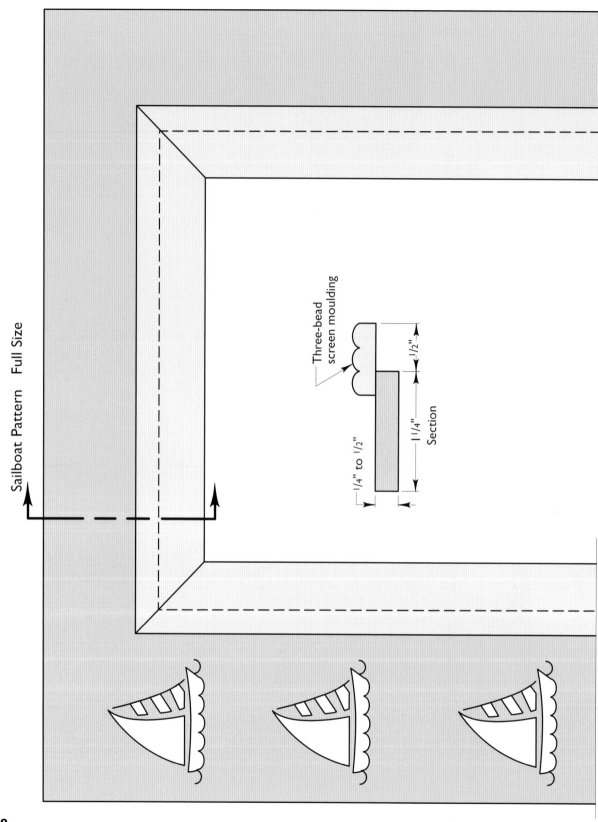

Sailboat Pattern   Full Size

Three-bead screen moulding

Section

1/4" to 1/2"

1 1/4"

1/2"

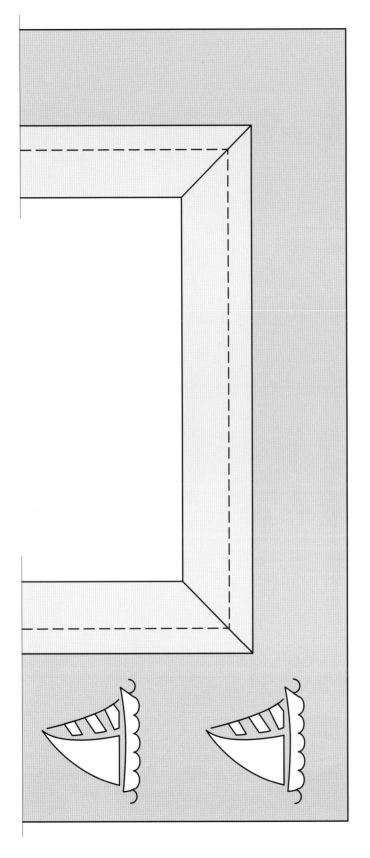

Sailboat

materials:

baltic birch plywood – $\frac{1}{4}$", $\frac{3}{8}$", or $\frac{1}{2}$" x
    $8\frac{1}{4}$" x $9\frac{1}{2}$"

cardboard for backer

instant adhesive or wood glue

sandpaper (100–150 grit)

three-bead screen moulding for overlay –
    $\frac{1}{4}$" x $\frac{3}{4}$" x $7\frac{1}{2}$" (2)

three-bead screen moulding for overlay –
    $\frac{1}{4}$" x $\frac{3}{4}$" x $5\frac{1}{2}$" (2)

instructions:

1. Photocopy pattern. Adhere copy to plywood. Cut out frame profile and openings.

2. Cut mouldings to length, mitering ends.

3. Glue moulding overlays onto frame, creating rabbet. *See Photo No. 14 on page 17.*

4. Sand and finish as desired.

5. Cut cardboard backer approximately $4\frac{7}{8}$" x $6\frac{7}{8}$".

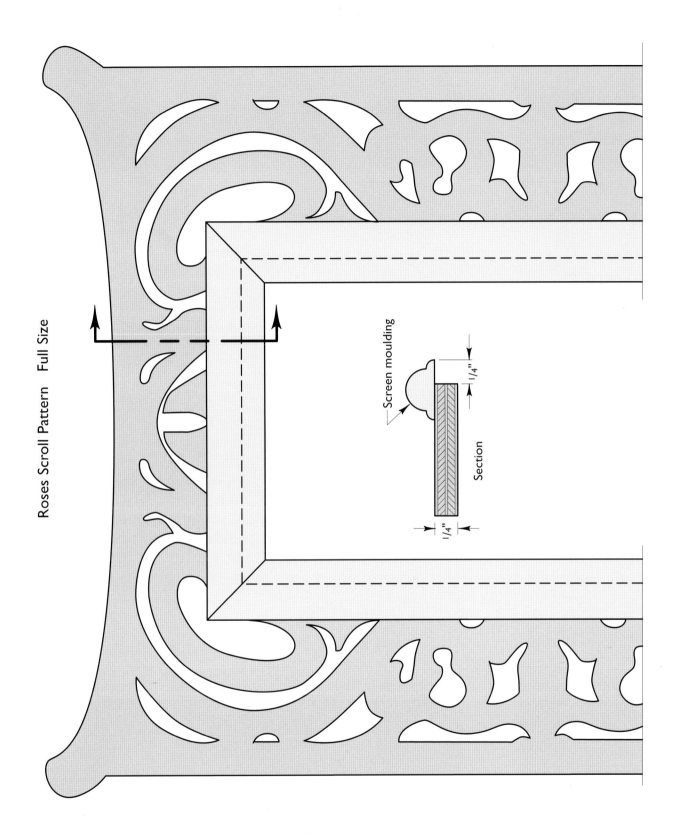

Roses Scroll Pattern   Full Size

Screen moulding

Section

1/4"

1/4"

Roses Scroll

materials:
cardboard for backer
instant adhesive or wood glue
plywood – $\frac{1}{4}$" x $7\frac{7}{8}$" x $10\frac{3}{4}$"
sandpaper (100–150 grit)
standard screen moulding for
    overlay – $\frac{5}{8}$" x $7\frac{1}{8}$" (2)
standard screen moulding for
    overlay – $\frac{5}{8}$" x $4\frac{1}{8}$" (2)

instructions:
1. Photocopy pattern. Adhere copy to plywood. Cut out frame profile and openings.

2. Cut mouldings to length, mitering ends.

3. Glue moulding overlays onto frame, creating rabbet. *See Photo No. 14 on page 17.*

4. Sand and finish as desired

5. Cut cardboard backer approximately $3\frac{3}{8}$" x $6\frac{1}{2}$".

Triangles Pattern   Full Size

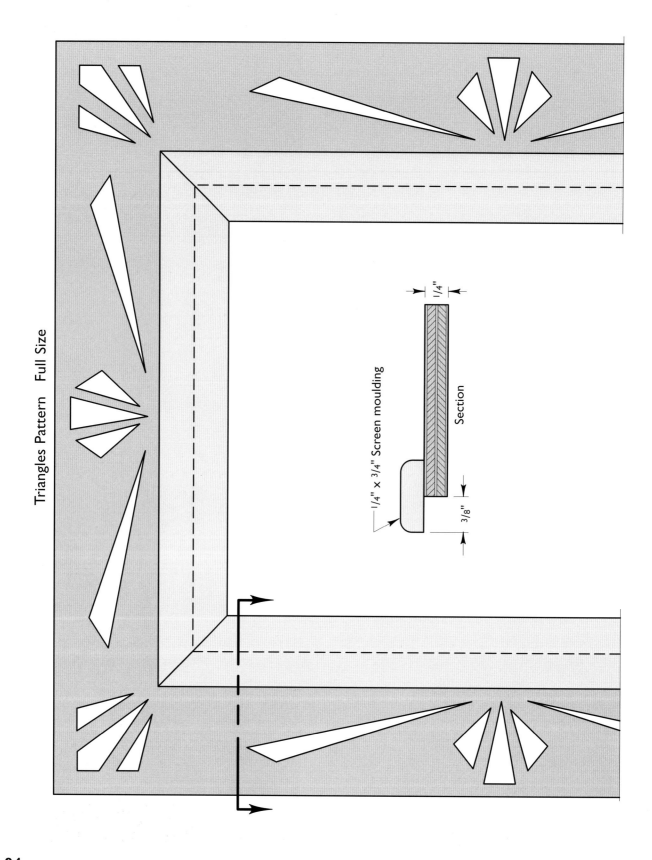

1/4"

1/4" × 3/4" Screen moulding

Section

3/8"

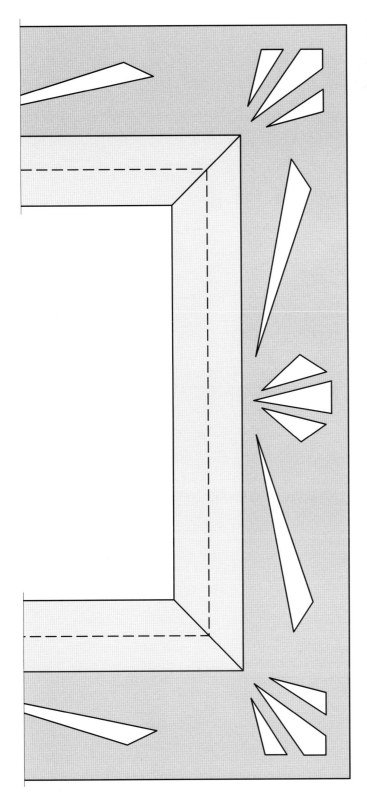

Here is a different way to complete this frame. Instead of gluing the moulding overlays onto the frame, the photo was placed behind the frame.

Triangles

materials:
cardboard for backer
instant adhesive or wood glue
plywood – ¼", ⅜", or ½" thick
sandpaper (100–150 grit)
screen moulding for overlay – ¼" x ¾" x 5½"
   (2)
screen moulding for overlay – ¼" x ¾" x 7¼"
   (2)

instructions:
1. Photocopy pattern. Adhere copy to plywood. Cut out frame profile and openings.

2. Cut mouldings to length, mitering ends.

3. Glue moulding overlays onto frame, creating rabbet. *See Photo No. 14 on page 17.*

4. Sand and finish as desired.

5. Cut cardboard backer approximately 4¾" x 6½".

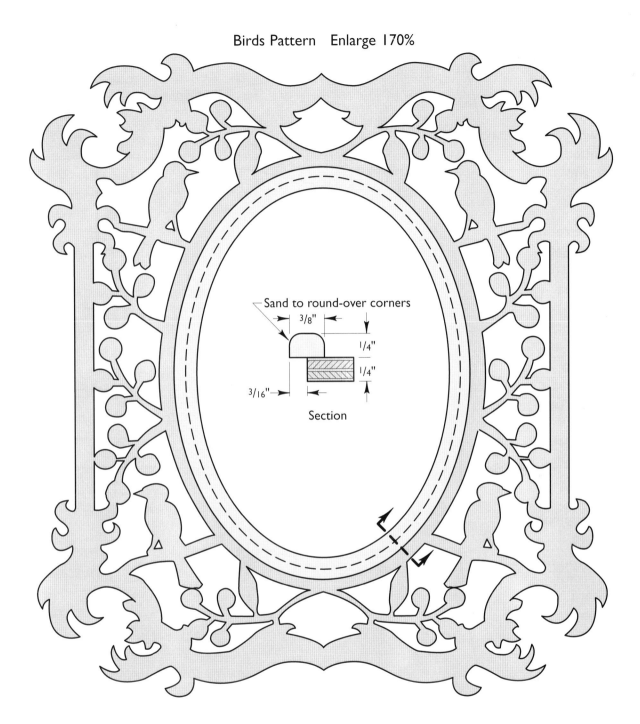

Sand to round-over corners

3/8"

1/4"

1/4"

3/16"

Section

Birds

materials:

baltic birch or hardwood plywood —
   1/4" x 10⅝" x 11⅜"
cardboard for backer
instant adhesive or wood glue

sandpaper (60–150 grit)
solid softwood for oval overlay —
   1/4" x 5⅝" x 7⅜"

picture frames

instructions:

1. Enlarge and make two photocopies of pattern. Adhere one copy to plywood. Cut out fretted frame profile and openings.

2. Adhere remaining copy to overlay stock. Cut out oval overlay.

3. Round-over oval overlay edges, carefully sanding by hand.

4. Glue overlay onto fretted frame.

5. Sand and finish as desired.

6. Cut oval cardboard backer approximately 5⅛" x 6⅞".

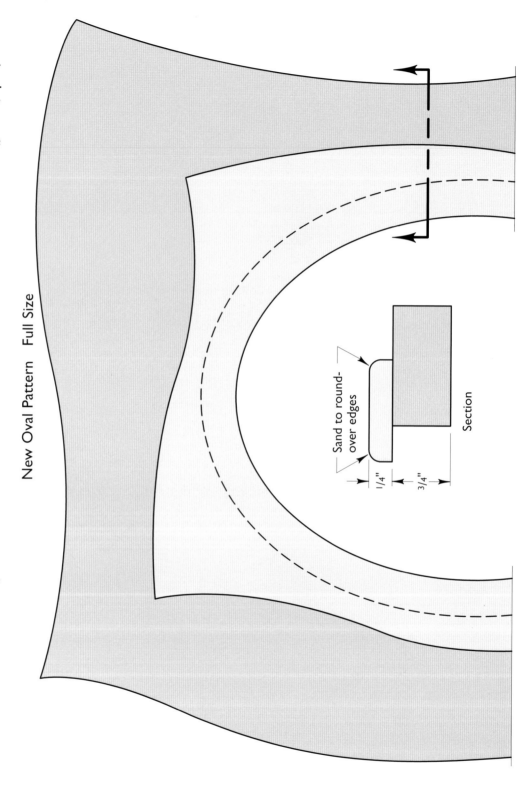

New Oval Pattern Full Size

Sand to round-over edges

Section

1/4"   3/4"

88

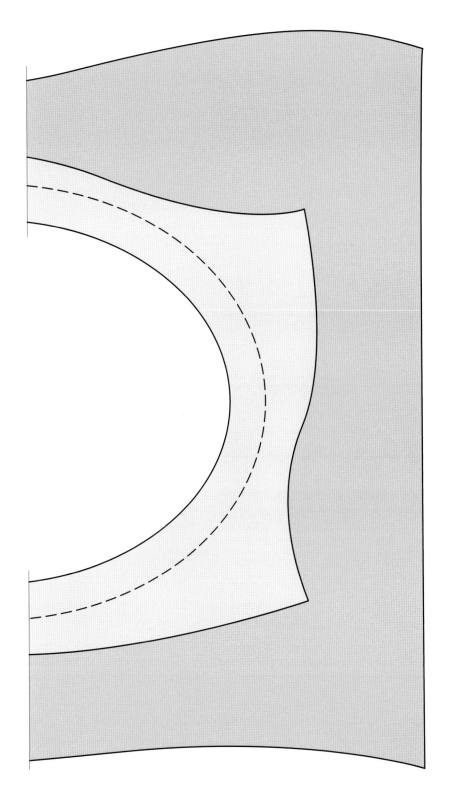

New Oval (photo on page 90)
materials:
cardboard for backer
finish — natural and black
hardwood — ¾" or ½" x 7¾" x
    9½"
hardwood plywood — ¼" or
    ⅛" x 5⅜" x 7¼"
instant adhesive or wood glue
sandpaper (60–150 grit)

instructions:
1. Make two photocopies of pattern. Adhere one copy to each wood piece. Cut out profiles and openings.

2. Sand and finish frame in natural, and overlay in flat black.

3. Glue overlay onto frame.

4. Cut oval cardboard backer approximately 4¼" x 5¾".

NEW OVAL

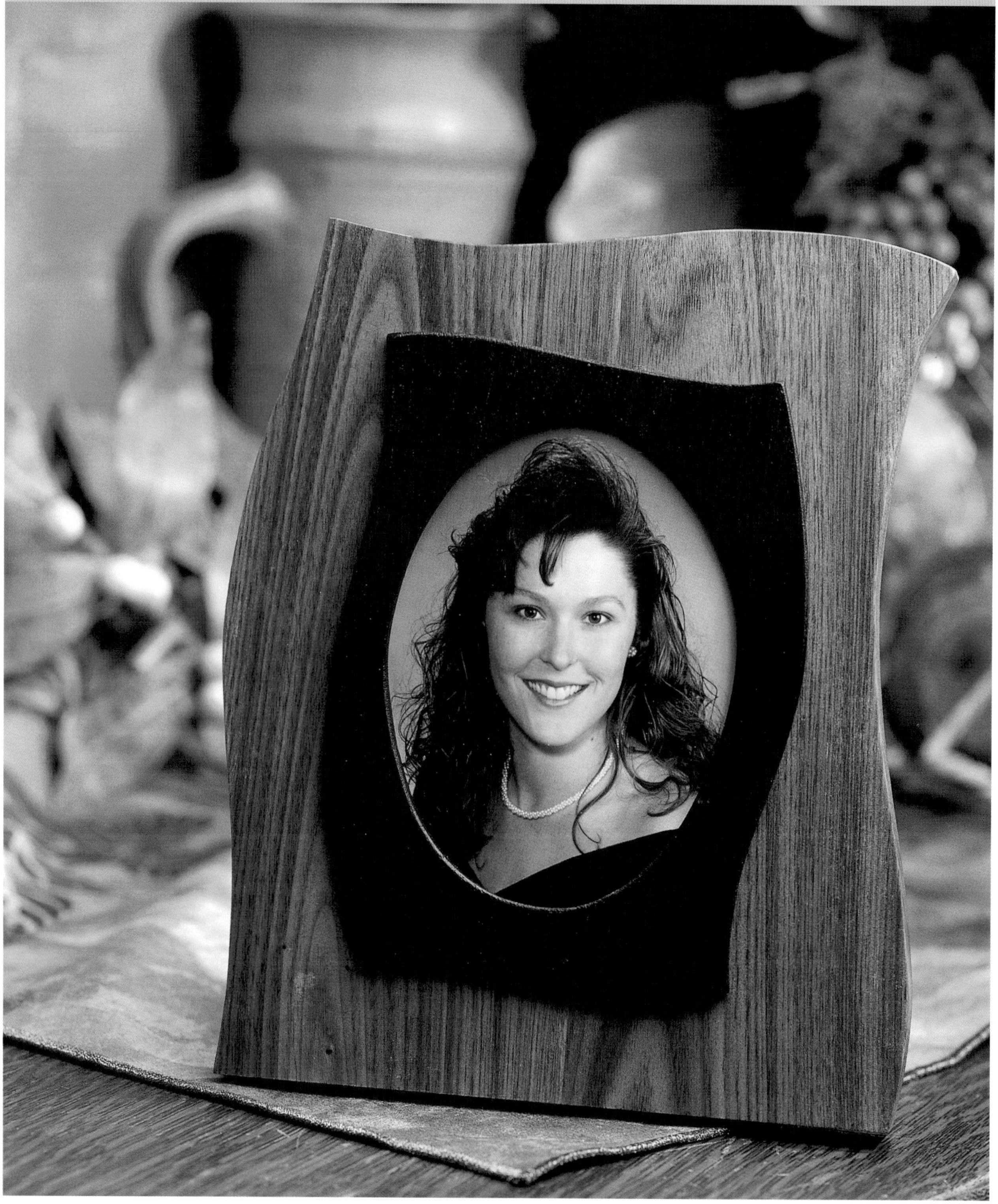

WESTERN MITER

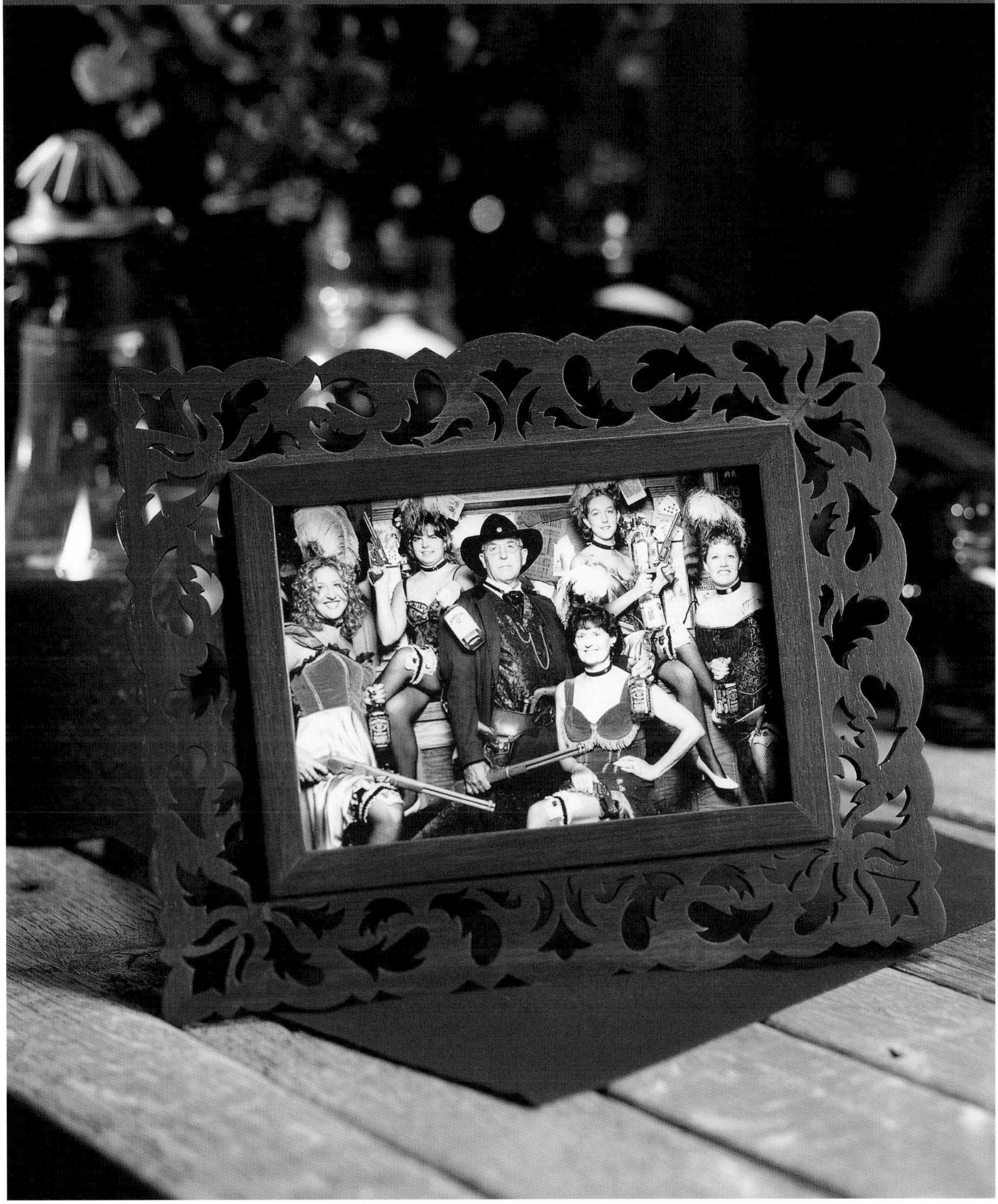

Western Miter Pattern   Full Size

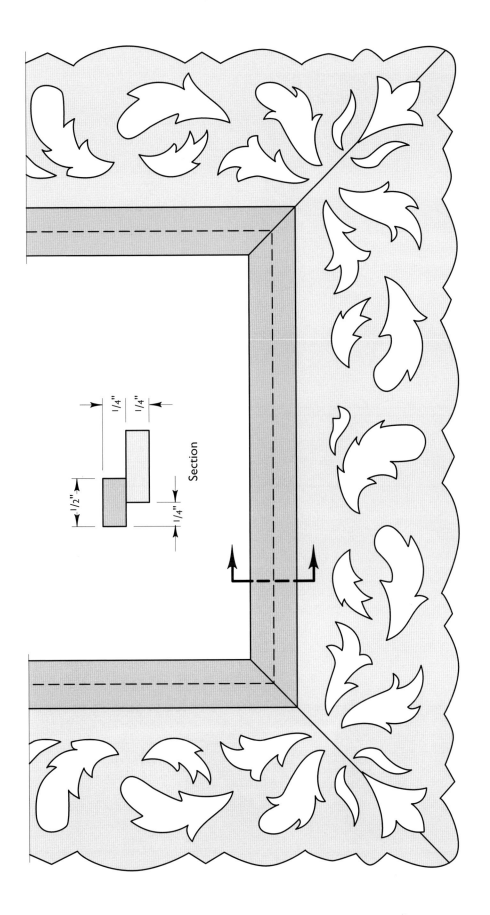

Section

1/4" 1/4"

1/2"

1/4"

*Tips: This frame
can be made in two
different ways, i.e., with
all the fretwork cut from
a single piece of 1/4"
plywood, or made from
four narrower pieces of
1/4" solid hardwood with
mitered corners. See
Photo No. WM-1 on
page 94. The following
instructions cover the
mitered technique.*

Western Miter

materials:
drill and 1/4" bit
instant adhesive
nails, 4d
plywood — 1/4" x 8¾" x
    12¾"
solid hardwood — 1/4" x
    2" x 12¾" (2)
solid hardwood — 1/4" x
    2" x 8¾" (2)
solid hardwood for
    overlay — 1/4" x 1/2" x
    5¼" (2)
solid hardwood for
    overlay — 1/4" x 1/2" x
    7⅜" (2)

instructions:
1. Cut four 1/4" x 2"
wide pieces to length
with mitered ends as
per the pattern.
Photocopy pattern.

2. Adhere copy to one long and one short wood piece, aligning the miters and inside straight edges.

3. Secure second piece of the same size under each pattern piece for stack-cutting identical parts.

4. Drill blade entry holes and cut out all parts.

5. Make test fit of mitered joints and adjust cuts, if necessary. *See Photo No. WM-2.*

6. Glue the fretted frame-work together at the mitered corners.

7. Reinforce the miter joints by gluing lengths of 4d nails across each miter on the back surface as shown in *Photo No. WM-3.*

Photo No. WM-1. This project has mitered corners to conserve as much of this expensive purpleheart wood as possible. The two long sides were stack-cut, one on top of the other, as were the shorter pieces to create identical parts. Also shown are the four overlay strips that are mitered and glued to the face (after the four fretted pieces are assembled) to form a rabbet.

Photo No. WM-2. Here is how to make perfect fitting miters. First, cut the miters as close as possible. Then check each joint with a square or draftsman's triangle. If there is any gap, hold the pieces together and make a cut through the joint. Do this once or as necessary until the joint fits tightly without any gaps.

Photo No. WM-3. Since it is nearly impossible to use mechanical fasteners to secure miter joints in a conventional way to join thin wood, and with only small surface areas remaining for typical gluing, reinforce the joint by gluing lengths of 4d finishing nails across the corners on the back surfaces with gap-filling instant adhesive.

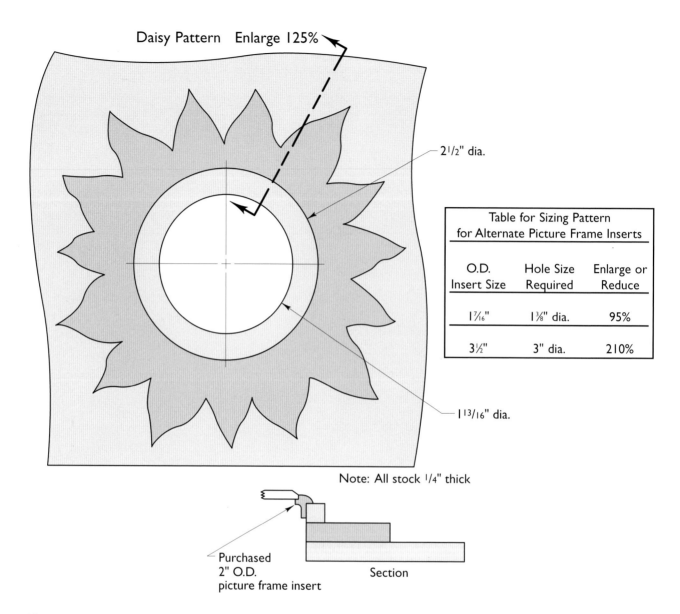

Daisy Pattern   Enlarge 125%

2½" dia.

1¹³/₁₆" dia.

Table for Sizing Pattern for Alternate Picture Frame Inserts		
O.D. Insert Size	Hole Size Required	Enlarge or Reduce
1⁷/₁₆"	1³/₈" dia.	95%
3½"	3" dia.	210%

Note: All stock ¼" thick

Purchased 2" O.D. picture frame insert

Section

Daisy

materials:
baltic birch plywood – ¼" x 5⅜" x 5⅜"
baltic birch plywood – ¼" x 4¾" x 4¾"
baltic birch plywood – ¼" x 2⅜" x 2⅜"
brass photo insert, 1⅝"-diameter
compass
instant adhesive or wood glue
sandpaper (100–150 grit)

instructions:
1. Enlarge and make two photocopies of pattern. Adhere each copy to larger wood piece. Cut out two larger profiles and their openings.

2. Layout top plywood ring with a compass. Cut out ring.

3. Sand and finish as desired.

4. Glue and assemble all pieces.

5. Install photo insert into frame.

Three-section Pattern   Enlarge 125%

Note: Vertical opening can
be modified easily by
changing the space in
this direction.

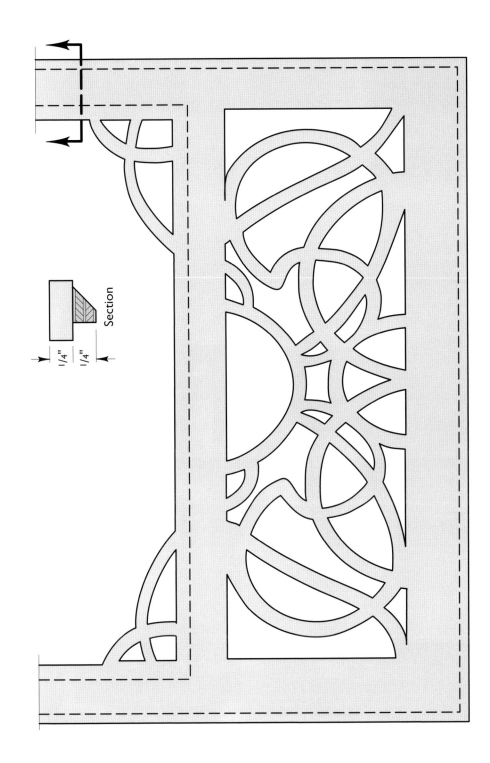

Section

¼" ¼"

Three-section

materials:
cardboard for backer
instant adhesive or
    wood glue
plywood or solid wood
    for frame – ¼" x
    8⅝" x 15⅛"
plywood for decorative
    back – ¼" x 8¼" x
    11½"
sandpaper (100–150
    grit)

instructions:
1. Enlarge and make
two photocopies of
pattern. Adhere one
copy to each wood
piece. Cut out profiles
and for each separate-
ly. Cut out openings
from wood for frame.

2. If desired, bevel the
outside edge of the
decorative back all
around to minimize
visibility of the edges.
*See Photo No. 16 on
page 18.*

3. Sand and finish each
wood piece as desired.

4. Glue decorative back
onto frame.

5. Cut cardboard
backer approximately
4¾" x 7½".

SHAMROCK

Shamrock
materials:
hardwood plywood – ¼" x 8¾" x 8¾" (2)
hinge
sandpaper (100–150 grit)
turn buttons

instructions:
1. Enlarge and photocopy pattern. Adhere copy to one plywood piece. Cut out profile and openings.

2. Carefully cut out a 4⅜" square from remaining plywood (back) piece to match fretted frame opening. Sand edges of square and reattach to back with a hinge. See Photo No. 25 on page 21.

3. Sand and finish frame and back in contrasting colors. Glue back to fretted frame.

4. Attach turn buttons to back around hinged square.

Flower

materials:
cardboard for backer
dye, paint, or stain
instant adhesive or wood glue
pencil
plywood for back – ¼" x 7" x 9⅜"
plywood for frame – ⅛" x 7" x 9⅜"
sandpaper (60–150 grit)

instructions:
1. Dye, paint, or stain surface of plywood piece for back. Photocopy pattern. Adhere copy to plywood piece for frame.

2. Secure both plywood pieces together in the inside opening waste area.

3. Stack-cut the profile and inside openings only. (Do not cut the design openings.)

4. Separate plywood pieces. Cut out design openings in plywood piece for frame. Sand frame piece as necessary.

5. Draw pencil line ¼" in from edge of opening circle of plywood piece for back and recut, creating a recess when both layers are assembled.

6. Finish plywood piece for frame in contrast to plywood piece for back.

7. Glue and assemble frame and back pieces together.

8. Cut cardboard backer approximately 4⅛" in diameter.

Flower Pattern   Full Size

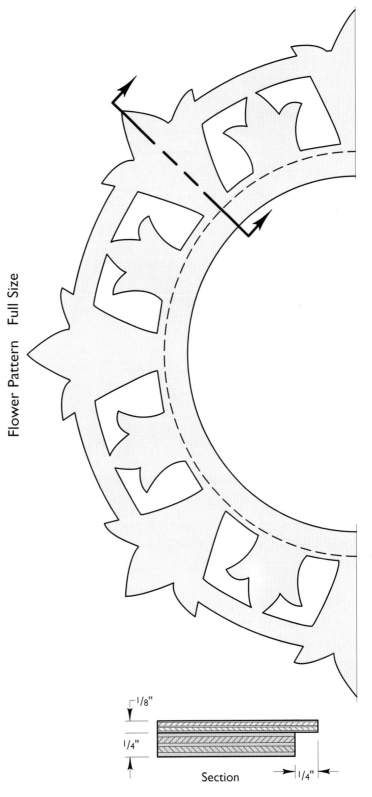

Section

⅛"

¼"

¼"

ARCHED FLOWER

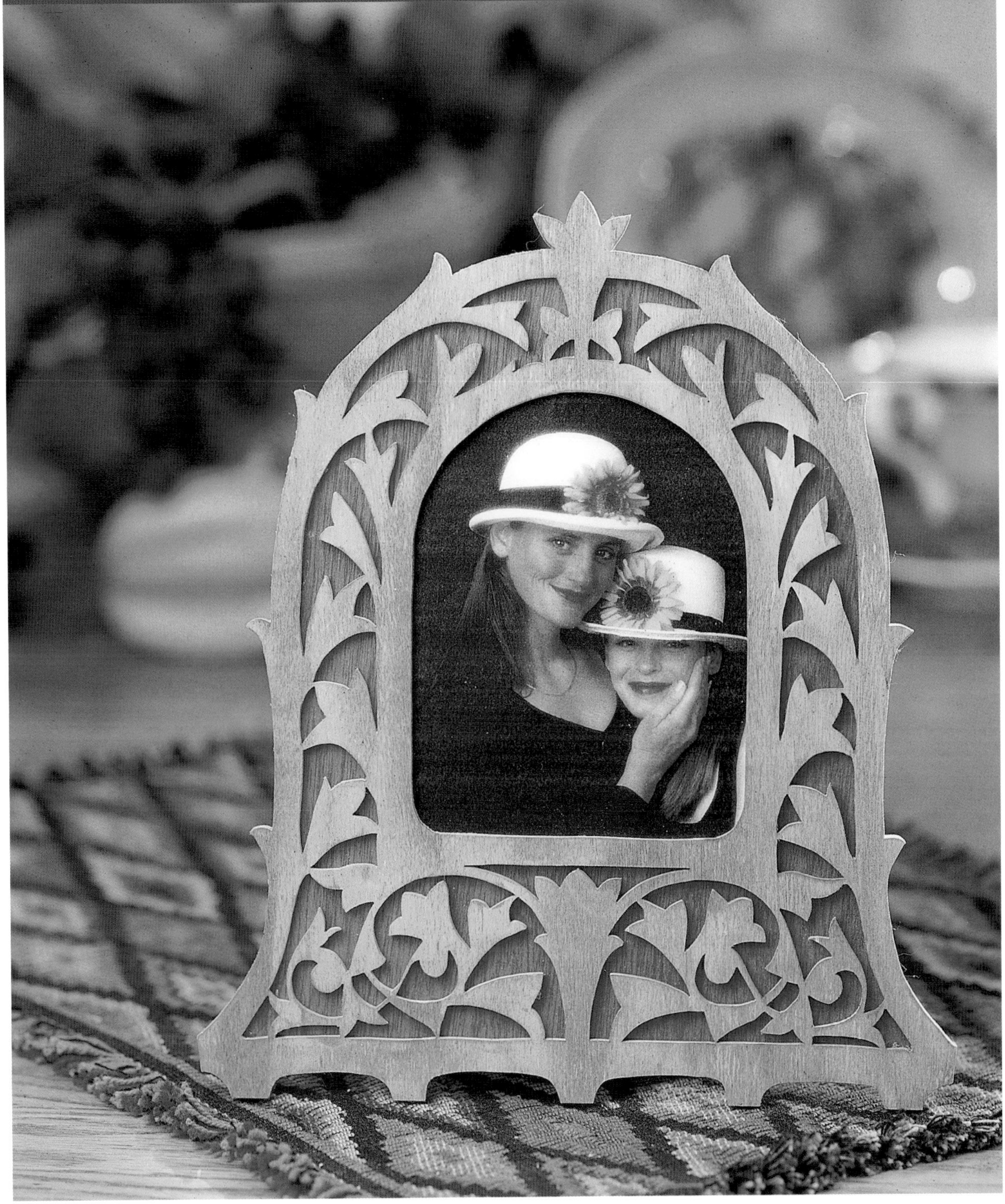

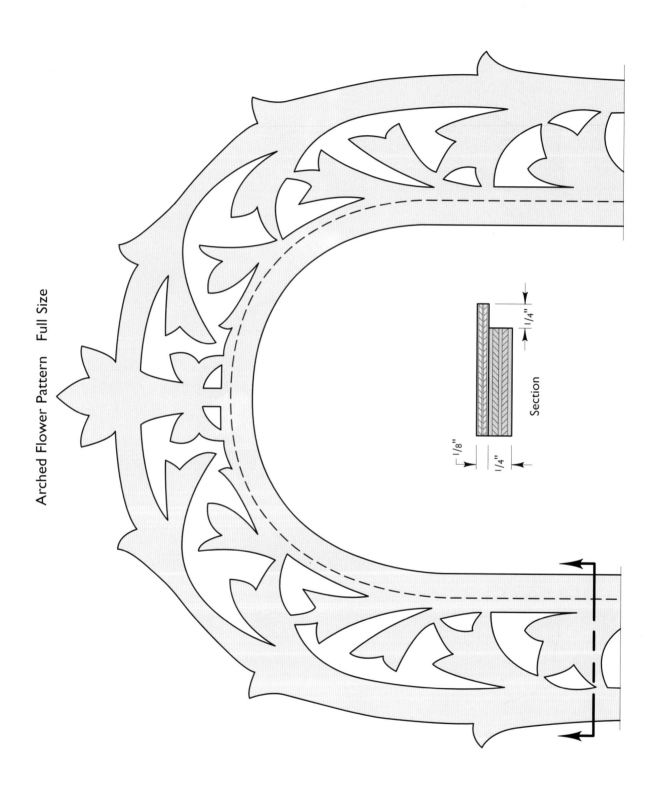

Arched Flower Pattern Full Size

Section

1/4"

1/8"

1/4"

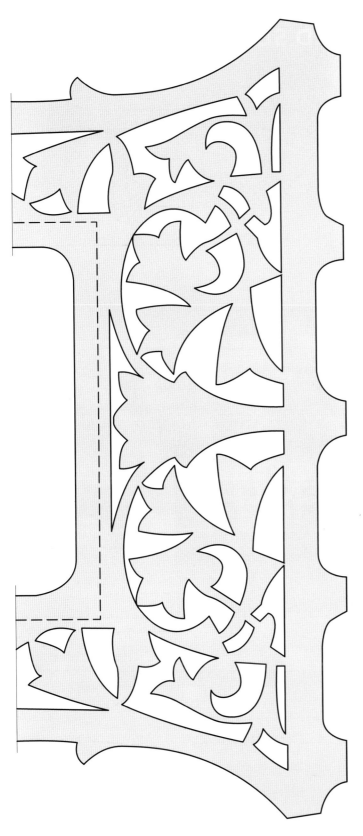

Arched Flower

materials:
cardboard for backer
dye, paint, or stain
instant adhesive or wood glue
pencil
plywood for back – ¼" x 7½" x 8¾"
plywood for frame – ⅛" x 7½" x 8¾"
sandpaper (100–150 grit)

instructions:
1. Dye, paint, or stain surface of plywood piece for back. Photocopy pattern. Adhere copy to plywood piece for frame.

2. Secure both plywood pieces together in the inside opening waste area.

3. Stack-cut the profile and inside openings only. (Do not cut the design openings.)

4. Separate plywood pieces. Cut out design openings in plywood piece for frame. Sand frame piece as necessary.

5. Draw pencil line ¼" in from edge of opening circle of plywood piece for back and recut, creating a recess when both layers are assembled.

6. Finish plywood piece for frame in contrast to plywood piece for back.

7. Glue and assemble frame and back pieces together.

8. Cut cardboard backer approximately 4" x 5".

Textured Slats Pattern

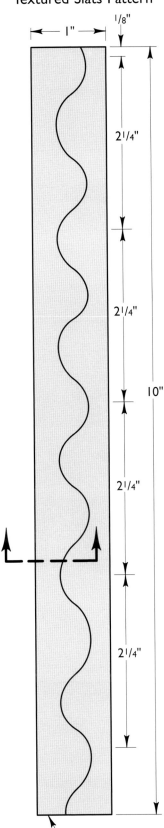

1"

1/8"

2¼"

2¼"

10"

2¼"

2¼"

2¼"

Enlarge 125%

Textured Slats Diagram

NOTE: ¾" x 1" x 10" (5)
Rip from flat sawn board

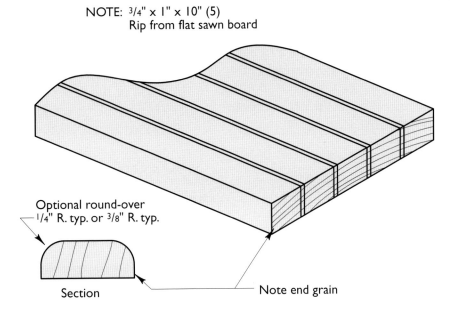

Optional round-over
¼" R. typ. or ³/8" R. typ.

Section

Note end grain

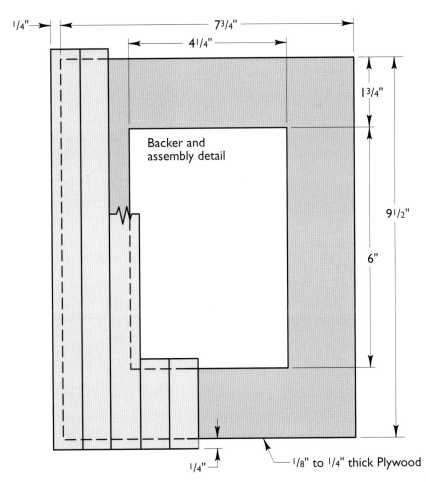

¼"

7¾"

4¼"

1¾"

Backer and
assembly detail

9½"

6"

¼"

¹/8" to ¼" thick Plywood

Tips: It is best to cut all of the strips from one board to assure uniform color and figure (grain pattern). A more interesting pattern will be created if all of the strips are cut from a flat or plain-sawn board.

Textured Slats

materials:
cardboard for backer
clear finish
flutter wheel sander
instant adhesive or wood glue
No. 2 shop pine – ¾" x 1" x 10"
    (5 strips cut from one board)
pencil
plywood for back – ⅛" or ¼" x
    7¾" x 9½"
router

instructions:
1. Photocopy pattern. Adhere copy to one wood strip. Cut strip into two adjoining pieces. Using one of resulting pieces and a pencil, mark each remaining wood strip for cutting. Cut each strip. *See Textured Slats Diagram on page 109 and Photo No. TS-1.*

2. Round-over edges with router and simple jig. *See Photo No. TS-2.*

3. Sand the sawn edges with flutter wheel sander. *See Photo No. TS-3.*

4. Cut three of the contoured pieces into 2¼" lengths. Make these cuts at the locations indicated to maintain the re-peating pattern. *See Textured Slats Diagram on page 109.*

5. Cut out rectangular inside opening from plywood back. *See Photo No. TS-4.*

6. Mark a vertical line ½" from one edge to locate the position of the first strip. Glue down the first strip and allow the glue to set. Then glue the remaining strips in place. *See Photo No. TS-4.*

7. Apply two or more coats of clear, natural finish.

8. Cut cardboard backer approximately 4¾" x 6½".

This easy-to-make textured frame shows optional ⅛" x ¾" contrasting strips fitted inside the opening.

Photo No. TS-1. One irregular cut produces two adjoining pieces for the frame face. **Tips:** Tracing a pattern piece with a red pencil is easier to follow than a black line.

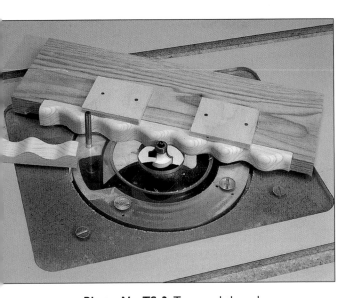

Photo No. TS-2. To round the edges, use a router table and the work-holding fixture as shown.

Photo No. TS-3. Smoothing contoured strips with a flutter wheel.

Photo No. TS-4. Glue the pieces so they overlap the edges of the plywood backer ¼" all around.

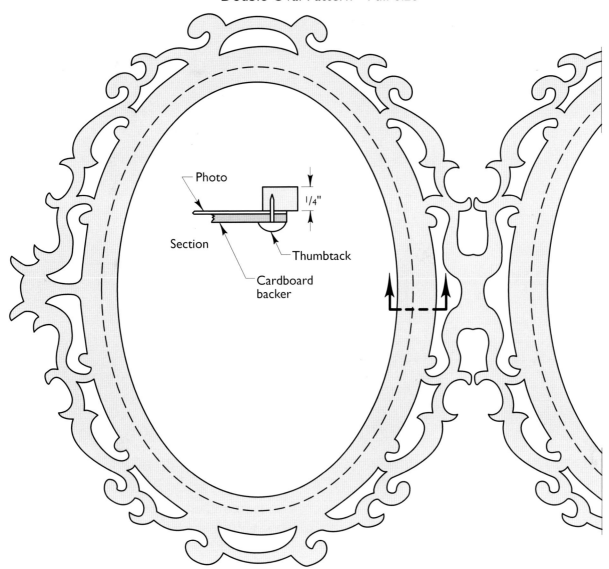

Double Oval Pattern   Full Size

Photo

Section

Thumbtack

Cardboard
backer

1/4"

Double Oval

materials:
cardboard for backer
hardwood plywood – ¼" x 6" x 10"
sandpaper (100–150 grit)
thumbtacks

instructions:
1. Photocopy pattern. Adhere copy to wood

piece. Cut out profile and openings.

2. Sand and finish as desired.

3. Cut oval cardboard backers approximately
3¼" x 4⅝".

4. Attach cardboard backers to frame with
thumbtacks. *See Photo No. 23 on page 20.*

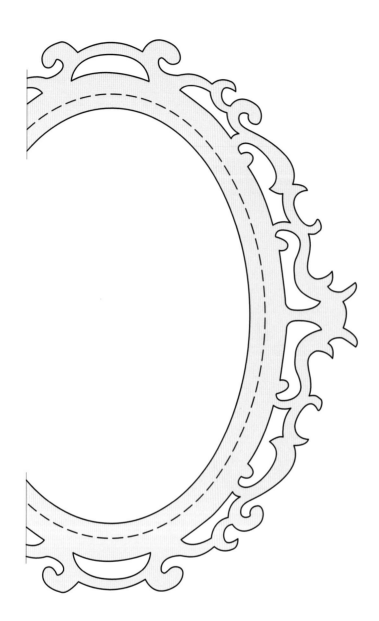

Skyline (photo on page 116)
materials:
cardboard for backer
instant adhesive or wood glue
MDF or plywood – $\frac{1}{2}$" x $6\frac{1}{2}$" x $8\frac{5}{8}$"
plywood – $\frac{1}{4}$" x $6\frac{1}{2}$" x $8\frac{5}{8}$"
sandpaper (60–150 grit)

instructions:
1. Make two photocopies of the pattern. Adhere one copy to each wood piece. Cut profile and openings from $\frac{1}{2}$" stock.

2. Cut profile and backer opening following dashed line of pattern from $\frac{1}{4}$" stock.

3. Glue layers together.

4. Sand edges flush and finish as desired.

5. Cut cardboard backer approximately $5\frac{1}{2}$" x $6\frac{7}{8}$".

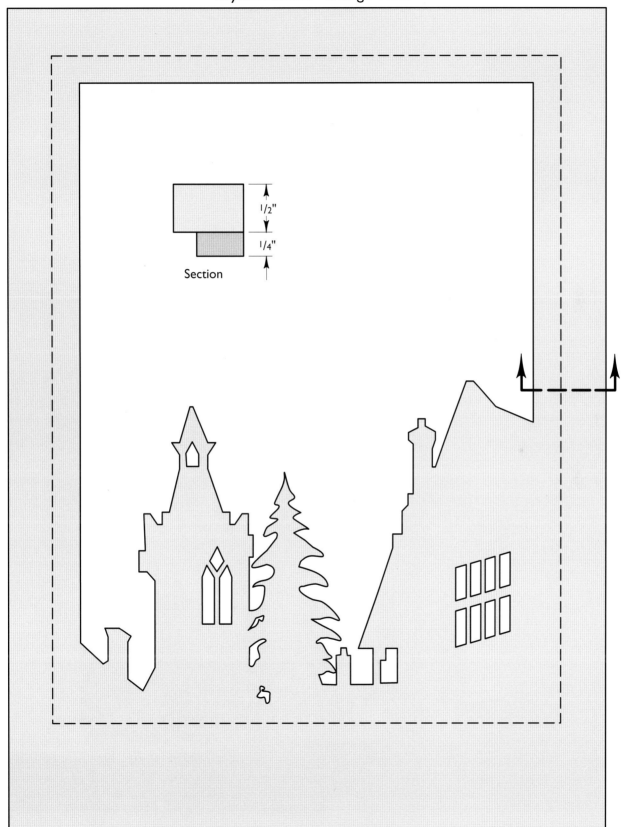

Section

1/2"

1/4"

5. Set saw table to desired angle. Drill a small hole at this angle for blade threading. Feed the wood piece into the blade in a clockwise direction to make the raised edge/back rabbet cut. *See Photo No. FF-2.*

6. Remove cut ring. Round-over outside edge of ring with sandpaper. Replace ring in back side of frame and push forward until secure. Glue ring in place in frame.

Freeform

materials:
drill and ¼" bit
instant adhesive or wood glue
pencil
router
sandpaper (60-150 grit)
solid wood scraps

instructions:
1. Cut away knots or other defects to make a freeform shape.

2. Draw a freehand shape for center opening with pencil.

3. Cut out center opening. Use this scrap wood to make text bevel cuts to determine the proper cut for the combined raised edge and back rabbet on inside edge of frame. *See Photo No. FF-1.*

4. Round-over inside edge of frame with router.

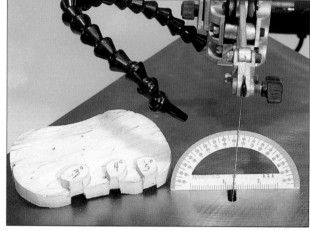

Photo No. FF-1. The cut-out center scrap is used to make test bevel cuts for the raised edge and integral back rabbet around the opening. Varying degrees of table tilt to the blade is what determines how high in relief the raised cut around the opening will be.

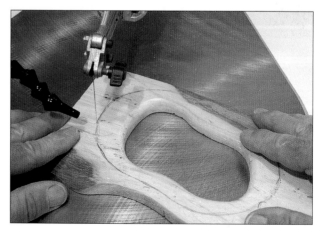

Photo No. FF-2. The table is tilted left and the wood is fed into the blade in a clockwise direction.

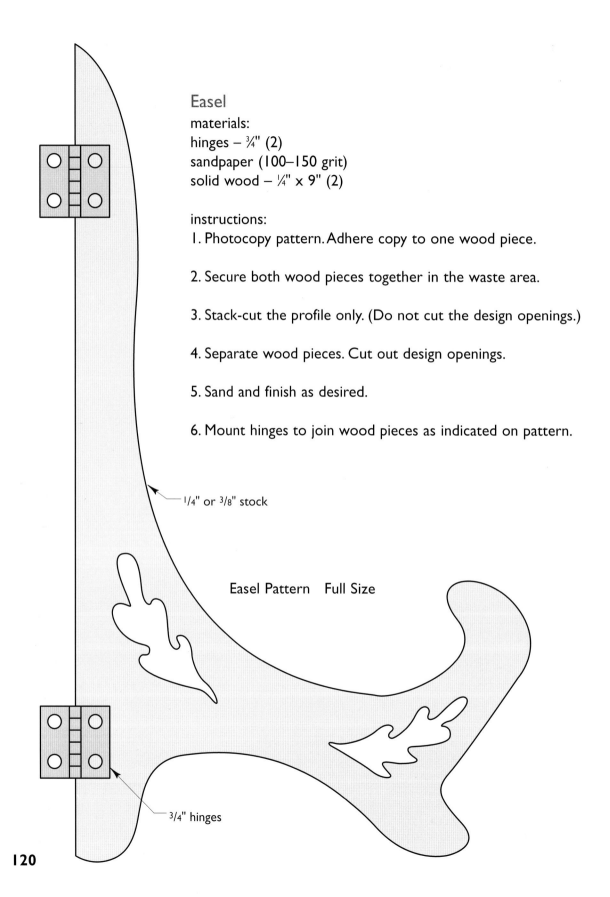

Easel

materials:
hinges – ¾" (2)
sandpaper (100–150 grit)
solid wood – ¼" x 9" (2)

instructions:
1. Photocopy pattern. Adhere copy to one wood piece.

2. Secure both wood pieces together in the waste area.

3. Stack-cut the profile only. (Do not cut the design openings.)

4. Separate wood pieces. Cut out design openings.

5. Sand and finish as desired.

6. Mount hinges to join wood pieces as indicated on pattern.

¼" or ³/8" stock

Easel Pattern   Full Size

3/4" hinges

Ornaments Patterns   Full Size

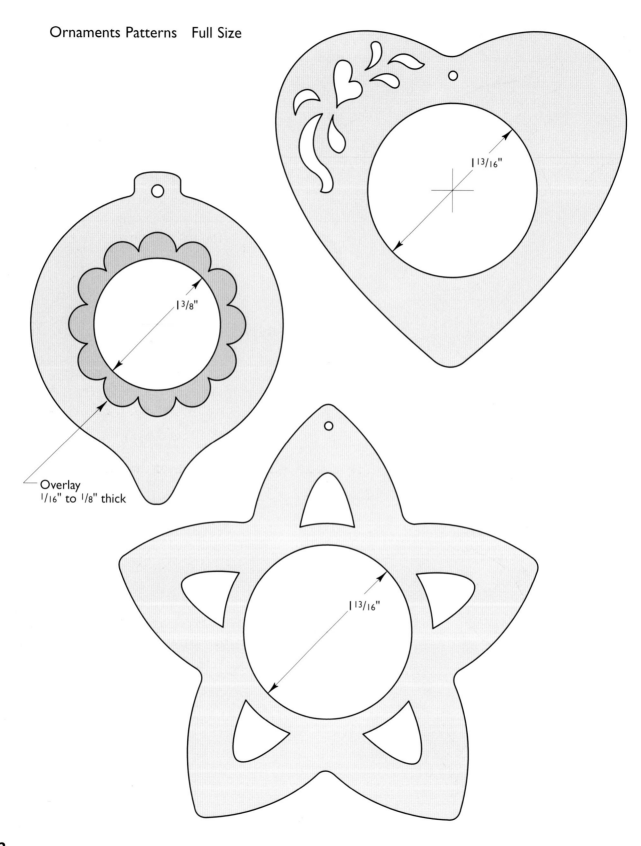

1 13/16"

1 3/8"

Overlay
1/16" to 1/8" thick

1 13/16"

Ornaments Patterns   Full Size

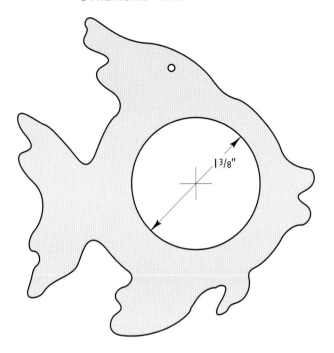

Ornaments

materials for one ornament:
baltic birch plywood – ¼" x 5" x 5"
baltic birch plywood for overlay –
   ¹⁄₁₆" or ⅛" x 2" x 2"
brass photo insert – 1⅝"-diameter
   for 1¹³⁄₁₆" opening; 1¼"-diameter
   for 1⅜" opening
cardboard for backer
drill and ¹⁄₁₆" or ⅛" bits
instant adhesive or wood glue
sandpaper (100–150 grit)
thumbtacks

instructions for one ornament:
1. Photocopy desired pattern. Adhere copy to wood piece. Cut out profile and openings.

2. Drill hole for hanger as indicated on pattern.

3. Sand and finish as desired.

4. Glue overlay onto frame if necessary.

5. Install photo insert into frame or cut cardboard backer approximately 2" in diameter.

6. Attach cardboard backer to frame with thumbtacks.

Magnets Patterns   Full Size

Magnets

materials for one magnet:
baltic birch plywood – $\frac{1}{16}$" to $\frac{1}{8}$" x $5\frac{1}{2}$" x 4"
magnetic sheeting with pressure sensitive
   adhesive backing
plywood for waste backer – 6" x 6"
sandpaper (100–150 grit)

instructions for one magnet:
1. Photocopy desired pattern. Adhere copy to front side of thin plywood piece.

2. Adhere magnetic sheeting to back side of thin plywood piece.

3. Secure thin plywood piece with magnetic sheeting side to waste backer. Cut out profile and opening(s).

4. Sand and finish as desired, avoiding finishes that may dissolve magnet's adhesive, such as penetrating oils or lacquers.

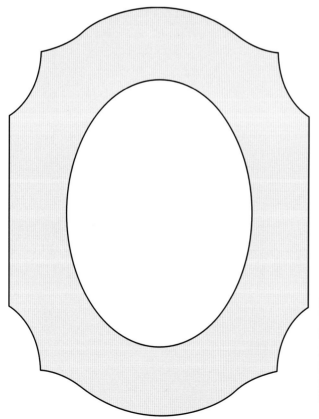

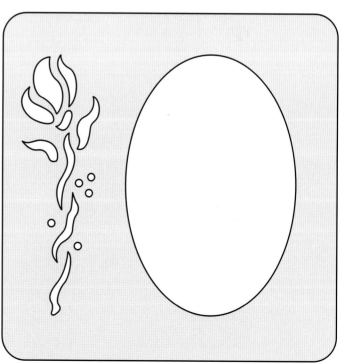

Metric Equivalency Chart

mm–millimetres   cm–centimetres
inches to millimetres and centimetres

inches	mm	cm	inches	cm	inches	cm
⅛	3	0.3	9	22.9	30	76.2
¼	6	0.6	10	25.4	31	78.7
⅜	10	1.0	11	27.9	32	81.3
½	13	1.3	12	30.5	33	83.8
⅝	16	1.6	13	33.0	34	86.4
¾	19	1.9	14	35.6	35	88.9
⅞	22	2.2	15	38.1	36	91.4
1	25	2.5	16	40.6	37	94.0
1¼	32	3.2	17	43.2	38	96.5
1½	38	3.8	18	45.7	39	99.1
1¾	44	4.4	19	48.3	40	101.6
2	51	5.1	20	50.8	41	104.1
2½	64	6.4	21	53.3	42	106.7
3	76	7.6	22	55.9	43	109.2
3½	89	8.9	23	58.4	44	111.8
4	102	10.2	24	61.0	45	114.3
4½	114	11.4	25	63.5	46	116.8
5	127	12.7	26	66.0	47	119.4
6	152	15.2	27	68.6	48	121.9
7	178	17.8	28	71.1	49	124.5
8	203	20.3	29	73.7	50	127.0

Index